RELATIONAL LEADERSHIP

A BIBLICAL GUIDE TO FELLOWSHIP

DANIEL C. JUSTER, TH.D.

WESTBOW°
PRESS
A DIVISION OF THOMAS NELSON
& ZONDERVAN

Scripture taken from the New King James Version. Copyright © 1979, 1980, 1982 by Thomas Nelson, Inc. Used by permission. All rights reserved.

WestBow Press books may be ordered through booksellers or by contacting:

WestBow Press
A Division of Thomas Nelson & Zondervan
1663 Liberty Drive
Bloomington, IN 47403
www.westbowpress.com
1 (866) 928-1240

Because of the dynamic nature of the Internet, any web addresses or links contained in this book may have changed since publication and may no longer be valid. The views expressed in this work are solely those of the author and do not necessarily reflect the views of the publisher, and the publisher hereby disclaims any responsibility for them.

Any people depicted in stock imagery provided by Thinkstock are models, and such images are being used for illustrative purposes only. Certain stock imagery © Thinkstock.

ISBN: 978-1-4908-6941-4 (sc)
ISBN: 978-1-4908-6940-7 (e)

Library of Congress Control Number: 2015904070

Print information available on the last page.

WestBow Press rev. date: 04/09/2015

CONTENTS

PREFACE TO THE INTERNATIONAL (2ND) EDITION

My book *Relational Leadership* has been a blessing to many leaders who seek to build strong congregations. Those who know me personally realize that I am very committed to universal truth and universally applied principles. Since the first edition of this book, I have traveled widely in the Messianic Jewish community in many nations. I have been deeply involved in new Messianic Jewish movements in Ukraine, Russia, Brazil and Argentina. I have been somewhat involved in Europe and South Africa. I am more convinced than ever that the basic principles of this book work in all these contexts. Where these principles are applied the movements are stronger, and where they are not they are weaker. In recent years, I have resided in Israel and believe that much of the weakness in the movement in Israel stems from a failure to apply these principles, though some are applying them to great advantage.

There are two very big issues that have become burdens I carry. One is the burden for the right government for New Covenant congregations. All kinds of congregations are valid: community congregations, house congregations, and mega-churches. All are capable of following the principles of *Relational Leadership*. However, the issue of right government is lacking in some quarters of the Messianic Jewish movement. I firmly believe that congregations are to be governed by a plurality of elders. This is the Scriptural norm, and no other government is found in the New Covenant

Scriptures. In any mix of elders, I believe a head or lead elder will arise. Such a lead elder is simply stronger in leadership, vision casting, programmatic implications, and enforcing the vision and program of the congregation. The lead elder and his plurality of elders should come to unity for any major decision. In unity, we have the blessing of the LORD for forward movement. Building a true team of elders is the beginning of a strong congregation. The elders cannot decide on a direction without the support of the lead elder, and the lead elder cannot decide on a direction without the support of the majority of the other elders. In addition, the congregation should confirm major directional decisions. In this, the congregants are validated as true partners and will be much more supportive of congregational directions. This form of government has not failed me for 40 years. Eldership government requires a real submission to the standards for eldership according to 1 Timothy 3 and Titus 1 (NKJV). It should go without stating that elders cannot be self-appointed or democratically elected. In the Scriptures, elders are always appointed by elders – and usually with an apostle in the mix of the ordaining of elders – or as the one who can himself appoint elders in pioneering situations. The pattern of self-appointment is a stunning anarchy that has become a pattern in the western world. A leader can leave one congregation, split from his past congregation and elders, and then set himself up as a lead elder. I cry out, "Where is there an example of such splitting and self-appointment to positions in the New Covenant Scriptures?!" Indeed, a person may be an elder, but to so split, and without the endorsement and confirmation of the eldership of one's congregation, such a split and self-appointment is anarchistic and rebellious. When a person believes they are called to plant a congregation, and they do not gain the support of their present eldership, they should transfer to another congregation. Only after a season of proving and relational building in the new community can they send them into a role of leadership planting.

The second matter of great concern is that in the Scriptures, congregations were linked together. Congregations were not independent. Eventually, elderships of the city formed with a city lead elder, called a messenger, in Revelation 2-3. Most scholars acknowledge that this person was the lead elder of the congregation in that city (Church of the City), called a bishop in the second century. I do not believe it was a monarchial bishop at this time. Cities were linked by apostles that traveled and could even form a council to decide major issues as in Acts 15. The idea of One Body, linked together, was common in the Reformation. It was not just a Catholic thing, but the hope of Lutherans, Reformed, and Moravians under the amazing Count Ludwig Von Zinzendorf. So I believe in linkage and that associations of inter-congregational leadership accountability are crucial. Association leaders form a court of appeal in major doctrinal and ethical disputes in the local congregation. These associations should be non-bureaucratic and led by a team representing a variety of gift ministries as noted in Eph. 4:11ff. They should give wide liberty for every congregation to develop its own style and program, and even to multiply naturally. They can strengthen each other through joint equipping efforts.

I am a firm believer in constitutional government. What do I mean by this? It is that the government of local congregations and associations of congregations should be in writing. Commitments, rights, and responsibilities should be clearly laid out. The extent and limits of authority should be clear. This is a great protection against both anarchy and abusive authority. Too many times I have seen congregations and networks blow up, partly because of a tendency among contemporary members of the Body to think that it is more spiritual to not put things in writing and to not have written covenants, constitutions, by-laws etc. It is thought that we can be so spiritual and that Yeshua will lead us by His Spirit. Our being so led is always a matter of partial discernment. I cannot tell you how many congregations have been saved from utter ruin because they had written constitutions that committed them to submit conflict resolution to a higher body in the association which provided a court of appeal. Without a written constitution, people assume levels of authority, and no one really knows where the real authority resides! I see such strength where there are such official associations as we have in the United States, Brazil, and to some extent in Ukraine. We have such clarity in Ethiopia was well. There is also a union of Messianic Jewish congregations in Russia with written standards. This is a great step forward for safety and progress.

So this book is now a reflection of over 40 years of leadership in the Messianic Jewish movement and in the Christian community before that. May it be of help to leaders and congregational members who are called to buy in to a leadership understanding.

INTRODUCTION

This book is my attempt to put the experience of over twenty years of pastoring into written form for the benefit of others. Some lessons were learned through difficulties and mistakes. Some were learned by the teaching and example of others. I do believe that the pattern of congregational structure put forth in these pages is Scriptural. It is a pattern that will work for large or small congregations. For the last twelve years, it has worked well in our congregations. These are congregations planted especially to win the lost sheep of the house of Israel. If it can work in this context, a field known for its difficulty, it can probably work in most other contexts.

Understanding leadership from a Scriptural perspective is not a strong point in the American Christian community. However, I truly believe that this area of teaching is one of the most important, for it is the foundation of congregational community. Our comprehension of what leadership is and does in congregational life will give us our guidelines for authority and submission, for fostering fellowship and evangelism, and for creating effective administrative structures. I hope that the reader will find that what is taught here is not too complex or difficult to apply. It is instead most natural. Unnecessary complexity and confusion arise from human foolishness.

Because I have pastored in a Messianic Jewish environment, I will be applying the teaching to that context. However, anyone in a culturally sensitive ministry can make many applications to their context. We do believe that there is a mandate from Scripture, to those members of the Body who are also Jewish, to maintain Jewish life in Jesus. Although Jewish life is ultimately rooted in Scriptural calling, all cultures have much that is good by the LORD's common grace. Therefore, varieties of New Testament faith expressions, according to different cultural contexts, are in my view willed by the LORD. May this book aid many in their endeavor to walk out their calling and service in the LORD's Kingdom.

Vision and Relationships

True success in congregational ministry requires putting forth a clear vision. If there is no clear trumpet sound, the people will not follow. Part of this vision should include the call to relationships as the foundational human purpose. Relating together is often called fellowship in the New Testament. The quality of life depends on the quality of our relationships. Relationships with people are the central meaning of human existence. Love is the center of fellowship. Common interests, personality compatibilities, and other human grounds for relating are secondary in the Scriptures. The primary factor in fellowship is to perceive the worth of people from the LORD's perspective and to identify with their uniqueness in His creation. This is an ability we receive only from the LORD. The New Testament in 1 John teaches that our love and fellowship with one another as disciples is based on our love for the Father – we love because He first loved us. Bonding occurs in the presence of the Holy Spirit that is unknown to those outside the Kingdom. Those who walk in the light will have fellowship with others who walk in the light.

The Central Life Purpose

This emphasis on fellowship among persons is made clear when we see that the LORD is a person who made us for fellowship with Himself. This is the number one relationship. As an old Christian catechism asked, "What is the chief end of man?" The answer was rightly given, "To love the LORD and enjoy Him forever." So Jesus taught that the greatest command is to love the LORD with all our heart, soul, mind, and strength (Mark 12). The second in importance is to love our neighbor as ourselves. This quality of love is not selfish attachment, but seeks the good of the other apart from self-centered considerations. The New Testament uses the word "agape" to describe this kind of love. Such love is eternal, for the LORD exists in three persons in eternal loving fellowship.

All other meanings in life – art, sports, physical pleasures, economic endeavors, and education – may be enhancements of life, but they are not the meaning of life itself. When a person has established a quality relationship with the LORD, he may be a candidate for leadership. However, if people enter leadership roles without this central foundation, their motivations will be off. There will be ego compensations; men will seek power, control, riches, and even sexual gratification outside marriage.

Life in the Kingdom

To enter the Kingdom of God one must come under the LORD's rule by being born again. In being born again, we are given the power of the cross to put to death the selfish center of our old life. We are given the gift of the Holy Spirit to enable us to love. The goal of the Gospel is to put everything right in a person's life by the power of the Holy Spirit. Through the Spirit, we enter into right relationship with the LORD. Through our fellowship with Him in prayer and worship, we are empowered to establish fellowship with others.

Marriage and the family are restored to true loving fellowship. Beyond this, the LORD establishes congregational community as part of human restoration. Fellowship in the congregation is a primary manifestation of the Kingdom of God. The goal of Gospel preaching is to expand the fellowship of the Kingdom to as many persons as possible. The Messiah Jesus prayed that we might love each other and be in the same unity as He and the Father. This was one of His last prayers before His crucifixion. There is a universal dimension to His prayer. How can I be one with all the members of the Body? I cannot personally know them. However, we do all share in the Holy Spirit. Through the Spirit we can be joined in a network of relationships of love. Every network can be linked to others, and all the members of the Body worldwide can potentially be in unity through the Spirit.

A Universal Vision

This idea of unity leads to the proposition that there is a common vision for all congregations. This common vision must be put clearly before the people. We exist as congregations to be a fellowship of mutual love. We exist to enjoy the LORD and one another. As part of this, we give ourselves to families and individuals that they might come into the LORD's order of restoration in fellowship. We seek to provide whatever healing through the Spirit we can so that everyone can enjoy fellowship with the LORD and others.

Expanding the Kingdom

The second foundation of the universal vision of congregations is to expand the Kingdom of God to as many people as possible. Congregants are to care for the lost and receive power and ability from the Holy Spirit to witness. The early disciples received power for witness when the Holy Spirit came upon them. Our witness begins where we live and work, but ultimately we should have concern for all people. To think we have "world concern" when we are not concerned with our neighbors is a delusion and a violation of the great command to "love thy neighbor." Therefore, a congregational vision includes this goal: to win the local lost people by individual, group, and congregational efforts. A Scriptural congregation also must bear a concern for world missions and connect to this in some significant way.

The universal vision of preaching the Gospel to all people includes a vision to reach the Jewish people. As seen clearly in the New Testament, the call to make Israel jealous by our witness is a call to all Christians, and not just Messianic Jews. No congregation will have significant involvement in all nations. However, according to Romans 11:11-15, the salvation of Israel is very weighty in its implications. All congregations are to have some kind of involvement in Israel's salvation, at least by prayer. I would wonder about the profession of a congregation to love the Jewish people when there is no allocation from its mission budget for this purpose.

To achieve the goals of congregational vision there should be home cell groups, inner healing groups, evangelism training seminars, witnessing campaigns, opportunities for growth in the prophetic ministries, mission's conferences, and much more. Beyond these universal goals, a congregation may find itself called to many special ministries of outreach – ministries of providing for the poor, witness through anti-abortion efforts, and establishing schools for educating children. However, everything must be ordered according to compatibility with and fostering of the universal vision dimensions of the New Testament.

In our own congregation, our vision has taken on a specific Messianic Jewish orientation. Our perspective on Messianic Judaism is that we are to provide a Jewish, Scripture-based expression of New Covenant faith. This is because we want to provide a context where Jews who believe in Jesus (Yeshua) are encouraged to worship in accord with the Scriptures. It is good for them to be in a place where they are motivated to keep their Jewish and Scriptural heritage along with their people. Secondly, we want to restore Jewish and Scriptural roots to the Church. We desire that the whole Church have a heart for the Jewish people. An enhancement of faith comes from understanding the Sabbath, fasts, and feasts of the Hebrew Scripture. Every congregation needs to expound a clear vision and the means by which they expect to attain their goals. Therefore, as an aid to the reader, I will try to clarify the vision of Beth Messiah Congregation, the congregation I led for many years. These values carry on today in the other congregations of Tikkun International.

The Experience of Beth Messiah Congregation: A Messianic Jewish Vision

This section will be especially relevant to a congregation seeking to put forth a clear Messianic Jewish vision. It will also aid any who are seeking to put forth a distinct vision for other specific callings.

Beth Messiah was a moderate size congregation by today's standards and has spurred the planting of several other congregations. We believe that the LORD is restoring Israel as a nation. Part of this restoration is His work to establish a movement of Jewish disciples that Paul calls "the saved remnant" (Romans 11:5). Paul makes it clear in this and other passages that Jewish members of the Body are still part of their nation and that the LORD's purposes for them are not finished. The expansion in numbers and maturity of this remnant will be a factor in leading Israel as a nation to turn to Jesus. This will usher in the resurrection from the dead (Romans 11:15). It is our goal to be a congregation that reflects these truths. Our evangelism is truly to the Jew first, but not to the Jew exclusively. We are committed to sending people to the land of Israel to minister the Gospel. However, we do believe we are called to fill the void of the lack of Jewish evangelism and understanding in the Christian community as well.

The Restoration of the Christian Community

Secondly, we believe that the LORD is at work in restoring the Christian community to unity, holiness, Holy Spirit power, and its Jewish roots of self-understanding. This is the implication of John 17:21. We believe that we will only see the nation of Israel turn to the LORD when the Church grows to the point of unity, power, love, and holiness. It will take this kind of power for the Christian community to complete its worldwide witness and to see Israel saved. Therefore, we are deeply, and with strong conviction, involved in praying and working for the unity of the Christian community. This involves inter-congregational prayer meetings between leaders and congregants in our county. We call these two parts of our vision "parallel restoration." The restorations of Israel and the Christian community are parallel, and they will eventually come together. We believe that such efforts at prayer and unity can bring revival to a locality. A revival can produce a great harvest. If there is a Jewish population in the area, this will greatly affect them as well. Our efforts at unity do not conflict with our Jewish calling. However, it is important that the congregation not lose its own Jewish expression and evangelistic edge by an imbalance in seeking unity.

Because we see fellowship as the foundational meaning of the congregation, we are committed to home groups, cell groups, or chavurah groups, or whatever name you prefer. We also teach that a congregation is not where a person goes to hear good messages. One can hear good messages on television and radio. We teach that a congregation is where one has fellowship and where one submits to be equipped to do the work of ministry (Ephesians 4:11ff.). All are to involve themselves in this work. It is also where one finds their primary fellowship commitments to the Body, where long term relationships are built.

Fostering Jewish Expression

In the history of the Christian community, there has been much misunderstanding concerning the Jewish people, including anti-Semitism and confusion concerning the application of the Hebrew Scriptures. Some of these confusions make the task of Messianic Jewish congregations difficult. These problems can be overcome if the congregation will put forth a clear theology of Jewish life and calling in the Messiah, the role of the Messianic Jewish congregation in this calling, and the place of the Gentile members in a Messianic Jewish congregation. We also need to include in that theology an understanding of the Christian community. We do not all need to live in strict conformity in a Messianic Jewish congregation. However, if there is no common theology and practice issuing from our vision, a Messianic Jewish congregation will soon fragment into factions, each with a different goal. These factions will ultimately cancel each other's efforts and render the congregation ineffective. Our publications *Growing to Maturity, Jewish Roots, The Irrevocable Calling*, and *Israel, the Church and the Last Days* provide the theology for our congregational vision. Beth Messiah requires every member to complete a study in *Growing to Maturity* and to affirm the basic vision and theology of that book. It would be well for every congregation, therefore, to choose and develop materials for its members, a "confession of faith," and a foundation statement for their agreed upon vision. This will prevent great problems from arising in the future.

In the last 20 years the American Messianic Jewish movement has seen a great influx of Gentile members. This can be a great blessing if they come for the right reasons. However, if they are there because they think the Messianic Jewish congregation is the ideal form, it will produce big problems. The forms of the Protestants are not at all invalid. All are not called to keep a pattern of Jewish life. Acts 15 and Galatians are very clear on this matter. The reason for Gentiles to join should primarily be a passion for the salvation of the Jewish people and a desire to be involved in such. They may enjoy Jewish life and culture, and indeed they should if they are called to the Jewish people. However, Gentile potential members should be tested in their motives – and attitude to the rest of the Christian community. They should profess that they are seeking to join primarily for a passion for the salvation of the Jewish people.

Messianic Jewish Theology and Practice

We present this information as a practical aid to congregations. Our intent is to move them toward a basic clarity of vision so they can come into unity in their congregational vision.

Our congregation is committed to the view that Scripture teaches the importance of Israel as a nation to the LORD's plan in salvation history. Romans 11:11 states in emphatic terms that Israel's stumbling is not permanent. The Kingdom will yet come in fullness, and Israel will yet fulfill its national destiny in the Age to Come. However, in this transitional age, the Gospel of the Kingdom will be preached in all the world as a witness to all nations. This raises several questions. What is the Gospel of the Kingdom, and what is the relationship of the Christian community to Israel?

The Meaning of the Kingdom in this Age

We believe that the Kingdom of God came to a greater extent in the ministry and teaching of Jesus. The Kingdom also broke into this age on the day of Pentecost (Hebrew *Shavuot*). It was the LORD's plan that there would be a stage of the Kingdom in which

Jew and Gentile would come under the rule of the Messiah. The Congregation of Yeshua invites all people to come under the rule of the King. Those who do so will have the privilege of being the Bride of the Messiah, the ruling Queen by the Messiah's side in the Age to Come. The Gospel, therefore, is the invitation to enter the Kingdom – that is, to come under the rule of the King. It is good news because when human beings submit to the rule of the King, their lives come into right order individually and corporately. The basis of this invitation is the atonement of Jesus. He died on the cross that we might be forgiven. We are transformed by becoming one with His crucifixion and resurrection that is expressed in water immersion (Romans 6). We can respond to the Gospel invitation and live in obedience to the King by the enabling power of the Holy Spirit. The Gospel includes the Kingdom elements of healing marriages, healing families, healing relationships, forming communities of love, and demonstrating the principles of the LORD in whatever life endeavors a disciple undertakes. The Kingdom is manifested in the life of the congregation, families, and individuals to the extent that they submit to the rule of the King. The coming of the Kingdom in this age is partial; the coming of the Kingdom in fullness awaits the return of the King. However, the return of the King awaits the completion of the task of the Body – to preach the Gospel of the Kingdom to every nation and to make Israel jealous.

As a manifestation of the Kingdom, we are a foreshadowing of the Age to Come. In the Age to Come, the LORD establishes justice over all of the earth. The Body is to be a community of love and justice under the rule of Yeshua through His designated, human elders.

The Jewishness of the Body

It is important to understand the Jewishness of the Body. Regarding Israel, Paul notes that Israel will be grafted back into what he calls "their own olive tree" (Romans 11:24). In Ephesians 2, the Body is called a commonwealth. It is a commonwealth of Israel. Rather than seeing the Christian community as something that has replaced Israel, we see the Christian community as something that grows out from the saved remnant of Israel. Those Jews who have believed are called the "saved remnant" of Israel (Romans 11:5). All true Christians are those who, through the message of the original saved remnant of Israel, have attached themselves to Jesus and to the saved remnant of Israel. Therefore, the Christian community is Jewish in its roots. It is a foreshadowing of the Age to Come when Israel and the nations will be one under the rule of the Messiah.

The Distinctive Call of Jewish Members of the Body

Israel, even in unbelief, is preserved until her re-engrafting. The gifts and call of the LORD to Israel are irrevocable (Romans 11:29). Someday the whole nation will call upon Yeshua. The witness of the whole congregation of Yeshua is an instrument in this. Until then, Israel remains as a sign of the LORD's faithfulness to His promises and in fulfilled prophecy by which she has been preserved and is being re-gathered to her land.

There are many Christians who agree with all of the statements we have made to this point. However, there is another crucial distinction in Messianic Jewish theology. It is that we believe in a distinctive call for the Jewish members of the Body – the saved remnant of Israel. This point is not seen by most Christian Zionists today. In Acts 15, the Jerusalem council released Gentiles from becoming Jews (being circumcised and keeping the whole Law of Moses) but did not release Jews from Jewish life as is sometimes thought. Acts 15 forbade Gentiles from committing immorality. This showed that the basic moral teachings of the Law were considered universal. After all, what defined immorality? Paul argues in 1 Timothy 1 that whatever is contrary to the Law in its moral teaching is contrary to sound doctrine according to the Gospel. Torah in its *universal precepts* is important and is to be applied by all disciples in the New Covenant. The Sermon on the Mount (Matthew 5-7) is a key passage in this application.

The Gentile members of the Body should be expected to appreciate the Jewish roots of the faith, while remaining a part of their nation, just as the Jewish members of the Body are still part of their nation. A Jewish member of the Body is also part of the one new man, the congregation of Yeshua (Ephesians 2-3). He is called a member of the saved remnant of Israel (Romans 11:5). This is also proven by the fact that Paul calls himself an Israelite (in the present tense) several times in the New Testament. In addition, Paul goes out of his way to profess his loyalty to his people and his continuing ethnic national identity in Acts 21. This profession of obedience to the Torah was made by Paul after the completion of his Nazarite vow (Acts 18:18) – a very Torah grounded thing to do!

The Jewish member of the Body therefore has a role to play in the destiny of the nation of Israel and the Jewish people. He is both part of the nation of Israel and part of the Body. He is one with Gentile members of the Body and one with the nation of Israel. Gentile is simply shorthand for those from nations other than Israel.

The New Covenant and the Mosaic Covenant

What defines living as a Jewish member of the Body in the New Covenant Era? The New Covenant promise is in partial fulfillment. The New Covenant will be fully manifest in the Age to Come. We believe that we are now under the New Covenant. It is important to understand how the New Covenant is different – and what of the Mosaic covenant is incorporated into the New. Drawing a correct contrast is crucial for the Messianic Jewish remnant. The New Covenant assumes the continuing validity of the teaching of the Mosaic material in the New Covenant according to 2 Timothy 3:16, where all Scripture is enjoined upon us for doctrine and practice. This verse was given before the New Testament was completed!

The primary contrasts between the Mosaic Covenant and the New Covenant in my view are as follows. First, the Holy Spirit has been poured out to all willing recipients to enable obedience to the commandments of the LORD. Jeremiah 31:31 speaks of the Law being written on our hearts. Ezekiel 36:24 speaks of us being given a new spirit and the Holy Spirit moving us to obedience. Second, the death and the resurrection of Yeshua fulfill the Temple-Sacrifice system so that the power of the benefits of the cross and the resurrection can be applied to our lives. This is the foundation of the New Covenant. Third, with the coming of the New Covenant, Jew and Gentile are made one in the Messiah. This foreshadows the Age to Come. Every Gentile can now attain to the highest place, being seated with Him in heavenly places at the right hand of the LORD (Ephesians 2:6). Every Gentile member of the Body needs to be taught that there is no higher status, including being Jewish, in the Body. This will preclude many problems of inferiority, misunderstanding, and of Gentiles wanting to become Jews within the Body. Being Jewish has a value regarding the LORD's historical purpose and distinctive calling, but not a higher status than being a Gentile. The LORD has arranged the drama of history so that Jews and Gentiles who are saved by grace will be humbled in their indebtedness to each other. The glory of the Gentile role in showing mercy to Israel will produce an indebtedness to the Gentile. This is parallel to the indebtedness that the Gentile has to the faithful Jewish remnant especially, but to the whole nation as well for the spiritual gifts that came to the World through Israel.

The Validity of Mosaic Teaching

Though we are not under the Mosaic Covenant, Mosaic teaching needs to be applied as is fitting to the New Covenant order. We believe that the universal moral teachings apply to all as demonstrated by Yeshua's teaching in the Sermon on the Mount. However, the New Covenant also promises the preservation of Israel. We therefore see one purpose of the Torah is to give us an understanding of Jewish life and calling. I use the Torah broadly here to include the teaching material from Genesis to Deuteronomy. It is in this literature that we find the basic vision of Israel's origin and destiny. Also included in the Torah are celebrations of remembrance that recall the LORD's mighty acts in constituting and in setting forth the destiny of the nation. The continuing validity of the nation of Israel implies the continuing validity of the celebrations and practices that are part of Jewish national life. This includes circumcision as part of the Abrahamic Covenant and the celebrations of the feasts, including the Sabbath as central to Jewish life and calling. All these are celebrated, with fulfillment in Yeshua being a most significant emphasis. There is also a prophetic "yet to be fulfilled" dimension to every feast. This is brought out in our book *Israel, the Church and the Last Days*. The Jewish member of the Body is the living bridge between the Christian community and the nation of Israel. The Jewish member of the Body is part of both. Important realities include identification with the nation of Israel, the Hebrew language, and knowledge of Jewish history and culture. Discernment is needed because not all that comes from the Rabbinic heritage is in accord with Scripture. However, we do want to be truthful in affirming that which is very beautiful in Jewish culture. Also our primary locus of identity, and meaning as Jews, must be Scripturally based. So in what way is the Mosaic Covenant superseded? It is primarily in the sacrificial system which is made very clear in the book of Hebrews. In addition, accommodations to that age in divorce, slavery, and unequal penalties for free people and slaves would not be in accord with the fullness of Torah in the New Covenant Scriptures. But most of the Mosaic material is made part of the New Covenant order.

Jews and Gentiles, One in Yeshua

A Messianic Jewish Congregation is one in which Jews and Gentiles join as one body with the task of preaching the Good News to the Jew first and also to the Gentile (Romans 1:16). It is one where Jewish members are encouraged to live a Jewish lifestyle in Yeshua. It is one where Gentiles join in and are enriched by being in a community where Jewish roots are visible. Jew and Gentile must be truly one. There are no barriers to participation or to leadership positions based on national identity. The Gentile is secure in his identity in Yeshua and does not seek to be a Jew. Our testimony that the Kingdom has come is that Jew and Gentile are one. Furthermore, both Jew and Gentile understand that their primary spiritual identity is that they are new creatures in the Messiah. This is their highest point of meaning and value. However, in the historical process of the LORD's plan, Jew and Gentile in the Messiah play different but complementary roles.

A Messianic Jewish congregation should be serious about all of the Scriptures, including the teaching of the Torah and the Prophets on justice. Yet there is a change in the way the Torah is lived in the New Covenant. Jew and Gentile in the Messiah are invited to the New Covenant Passover Seder because of the Messiah's sacrifice. In the first century, Gentiles were excluded. Ephesians makes it clear that this is no longer the case. There were accommodations in the Mosaic Covenant for a people who did not all have the opportunity to be filled with the Spirit. Yeshua precludes divorce for all but the most severe situations. Moses allowed it. At the same time, though the Age to Come will see a universal Sabbath observance, there is an accommodation for this age. In this age, Gentiles are not required to keep the seventh day as their Sabbath, as long as they keep some day as separate unto the LORD (Isaiah 66, Romans 14). In a Messianic congregation, we should be serious about the Torah and study each verse, asking how it should be applied in the New Covenant order. The Holy Spirit will lead us to further understanding.

Evangelism and Cultural Identity

While a Messianic Jewish congregation is a home for people from many ethnic groups, our primary emphasis in evangelism is to the Jewish people. This is not the only thrust, as we are involved in world missions. While we seek to make all people feel at home, our primary emphasis is to provide a context where Jewish people feel at home. The foods we serve at our gatherings and the dances we learn are expressions of this calling. The music we use is part of this too. Our Jewish members are encouraged to continue to live a Jewish lifestyle for the salvation of our people and the enrichment of the congregation. Jews and Gentiles in our congregation are also encouraged to involve themselves in the Jewish community and to befriend Jewish people.

Living a Jewish lifestyle is a communal experience. Our congregation tries to provide a communal context in which one can express his Jewishness. Living as a Jewish family can be done in a Christian congregation that does not have a place for Jewish roots, but it is more difficult. A Jew can also be called to a mission field other than the Jewish vineyard; if Paul could do it, so can others. On the other hand, most will become culturally oriented according to the community to which they belong.

Our congregation sees itself as playing a last days' role in restoring Jewish roots (contextual and Scriptural understanding) to the Christian community and preaching the Gospel to the Jewish people. We believe that this is preparation for Israel's calling upon Yeshua and hastening His return (Matthew 23:39, Romans 11:14-15).

Unity of Vision

It is crucial that these distinctives that express our vision be clearly seen and affirmed by those who become full members of our congregation. This is accomplished by fully putting forth the congregational vision on a regular basis. It should be periodically reaffirmed in public preaching. We want our members to be excited about these distinctives and our fostering of their application in the community. When a congregation does not clarify its vision in public preaching and in membership classes, or by other means so that there is unity in the vision, it is headed for division. Many will come because the music is good, or they like the freedom expressed in Messianic Jewish dance, or the preaching is good. However, this is not a sufficient basis for membership. Full membership is reserved for those who fully affirm the vision and are willingly built into a community with others to fulfill that vision. Without a unity in vision and direction, the members will eventually undercut one another. We have found this to be a significant problem in many congregations.

One way we have found to help people come to unity of vision is through provisional membership. For example, we are not congregations that are heavily into Rabbinic practice and prayer. We do include Rabbinic prayer expression, but we equally include modern Messianic Jewish expressions in worship. Those who desire a traditional Rabbinic service will find themselves dissatisfied because we have not defined our primary Jewish identity by Rabbinic observance. In addition, those who want to reject Rabbinic expression will find themselves struggling in our congregations. Traditional worship expressions do have a significant part in our services. We have a provisional membership for those who want to be submitted to authority while they search out the issues and decide whether they are called into our community. Full membership, however, requires a full affirmation of this basic vision. If people cannot come to unity behind our basic vision, then they are encouraged to be committed elsewhere.

When we first did this at Beth Messiah in the 1980s, we lost many people who did not affirm our vision and values. However, we gained a greater unity and more long term progress. Congregations that are not Messianic Jewish also need to set forth their visions, distinctives, goals, and expectations so that those who join will be working in unity with the goals of the leadership.

CHAPTER 1

The Claim of the Kingdom of God

American Christianity has put forth an "easy believe-ism" that has undercut the Scriptural mandate to build disciples of strong commitment and character. If we are to see congregations built that are in line with the heart of the LORD, the orientation of American Christianity must be resisted. The claim of the Kingdom of God upon a person's life becomes known when the Gospel of the Kingdom is rightly preached. Yes, it is by believing that we are saved. However, this must be put into a larger context of both what the Scriptures mean by faith or believing and what the Gospel of the Kingdom is.

The Good News of the Kingdom of God is the undeserved invitation to return to the house of the Father or the realm of the King. It is an invitation to come under the rule of a just and good King. We are called to leave the realm of the rule of the devil, the god of this world, and to enter the Kingdom of God. How do we enter this Kingdom? It is by believing and making a faith-trust commitment to the King. Yeshua died for our sins so that we might enter the Kingdom and be filled with the Spirit. The Spirit is the LORD's own life in us. This life enables us to live in obedience to the King. The motive for obedience is a relationship of trust and love. We place our trust in His grace to enable, not our own fleshy attempts at good works. By this Paul can say in Romans 3:31 that faith establishes the law. This faith commitment is also expressed in water immersion where the person experiences a co-death and resurrection in Yeshua. The person is transformed and now able to obey the Torah of Yeshua.

Kingdom Restoration in Every Sphere of Life

The claim of the King upon a person's life is total. In return, we gain the benefit of life under the rule of a good King, a King who puts everything right in a person's life. There is substantial healing in the Kingdom, both physical and spiritual. There is a promise of provision for all our material needs if we seek the Kingdom first (Matthew 6:33). There is a restoration of the relational meaning of life: with the LORD, in marriage, family, friendships, and the establishing of community in congregational life. Alienation is overcome. The good gifts of the LORD's creation are enjoyed in their proper usage. Furthermore, there is a destiny of great purpose for every disciple. Ultimately, life under the rule of the King is manifest in individuals, families, and communities. Our witness to the King's greatness becomes evident in the business, political, educational, and artistic worlds. The present stage of the coming of the Kingdom is always partial. Full manifestation of the Kingdom awaits the return of Yeshua. The benefits of the Kingdom today pale in the light of the Kingdom life we will enjoy forever in the ages to come. As Scripture says, eye has not seen nor ear heard, nor can the mind of man comprehend the riches that the LORD has in store for Yeshua's disciples (1 Corinthians 2:9; Isaiah 64:4, 65:17).

Kingdom Warfare

This present stage of the Kingdom is a stage of warfare with the kingdom of darkness. This is not the age in which we can take our ease in Zion! Therefore, although there are such benefits in life in the Kingdom that all rational people should choose it, it should be clear that we are in a war with trials, tribulations and casualties. This is a manifestation of the partial quality of the reality of the Kingdom during this transitional age. Our task is to engage in this warfare and to rescue people and societies from the kingdom of darkness. When the Gospel of the Kingdom has been adequately preached in all the world as a witness with powerful signs and wonders that manifest Kingdom power, then the end will come; Yeshua will return. A significant part of this mandate is to make Israel jealous. I am aware that some of this is an extension of the last chapter, but it is so central in what the LORD is seeking to build.

Thy Kingdom Come

When we pray, "Thy Kingdom come, Thy will be done, on earth as it is in heaven," we are asking for what is central to the heart of the LORD. We are praying, "Establish Your righteous rule in me, in my family, in my congregation, and in every realm of life that I touch. In establishing Your rule in the Body, hasten the day that the whole world will come under the rule of Jesus!" This should be the desire of every disciple of Jesus. If we are to have vibrant and effective congregations from the LORD's point of view, then this must be our emphasis in preaching and teaching in our community celebrations, in our education classes, and in our small group ministries. It is important to note what the LORD sees as an effective congregation. It is not the place where the greatest rally and Messianic Jewish or Christian entertainment is provided Saturday or Sunday morning. Our values must change if this is what we think! It is a place where community under His rule is built. There is fervent commitment to the LORD in the community, and all are equipped to fulfill their destiny in witness and vocation. It is where lives are healed.

Holiness in Congregational Life

All progress depends on first producing a core of people who are all out for the Kingdom of God. When this is the case, then we can call people into significant roles of sacrifice, both in servant leadership or in other roles of service.

If we are to see our communities under the favor of the LORD, our preaching must build holiness in our people. By the anointing of the Spirit, we must inspire them to whole hearted commitment to the Kingdom of God and to repentance from sin and worldliness (Scripturally defined). We must inspire them to be as useful as they can possibly be to the purposes of the LORD so that they might fulfill their destiny. To spur this, we must lift up Yeshua in our preaching so people are stimulated to love Him. The devotional life must be taught. A deep devotional life must be characteristic of our people. When this is in place, we are ready to do the works of the Kingdom of God. The LORD's claim is total. The pleasures of this world system must become unattractive. The LORD will give us many opportunities to freely enjoy the many gifts of His creation, but this must be at His behest, not by our own willfulness. We are to walk in the Spirit, in a constant sense of His presence. Then our desires will be in Him and His desires will be our desires. It is crucial to build up our people in faith confidence to believe the promises of the LORD and overcome in every challenge of life. We find this emphasis is important today because people are so fearful. Also, we live in a country where scientific humanism pervades making belief difficult. People need a lot of building up; we need to preach faith.

Discipleship that emphasizes these themes causes people to want to be effective witnesses and to be examples of the LORD's righteous rule. One comes to delight in showing forth the LORD's righteous rule in every challenge; our responses show forth His love, justice, meekness, gentleness, firmness, and patience. We truly trust Him! Obviously while we seek a Jewish expression of our faith, this Jewish expression is not the center. The center of the picture must be the Messiah Jesus.

Vision for Planting Congregations

My own vision of congregational planting is not to first draw a large crowd. It is rather to emphasize a home group structure. Perhaps a home group will be the first step. If there is a larger celebration, fifty people are enough to begin that with. This core must be trained in the vision and commitment of the Kingdom. Out of this core will arise our first leaders. One of the most important tasks of the planter, or the leader who is seeking to bring reformation to a larger group, is to identify those whom the LORD has chosen to be trained as leaders. They will be those who excel in response to the Kingdom message and the joy of commitment.

Leadership Standards

The prayer and effort of the head leader should issue from a clear focus on expanding leadership (elders and deacons). The Kingdom of God can only expand through a congregation to the extent of the increase of qualified leaders. These leaders must relate in a quality way to the LORD and to others. In John 15:1-7, Yeshua taught that unless we abide in the vine, we can do nothing. The abiding life in Jesus is the key to bringing forth much fruit. The central key in bringing forth leaders is to inspire them toward the abiding life. Potential leaders are those who have attained to the abiding life. Unless this is attained, all other natural gifts are inconsequential.

Indeed, great natural gifting apart from the abiding life might lead the pastor to wrongly place people in leadership. He can give a leadership position to one who is not qualified by the LORD's standards.

The relational quality of a person's life is clearly the foundation for leadership. Other gifts and talents may be needed but the quality of one's relationship with the LORD and others is the test of tests. What is their marriage like? How is their family life? What is the quality of friendships? Is this a person that can enter long-term friendships? Is there stability in all of this? There may be many other developmental needs in a person's life, but if these things are solid, everything else will fall into place. I will go over the Scriptural standards for leadership in greater depth in a later chapter.

At this point, I simply want to stress why this relational dimension is so crucial. The works that are pleasing to the LORD and produce lasting fruit are works of faith. Works of faith can only be produced out of a love relationship with Yeshua. The power of the soul, as Watchman Nee noted, can use human charisma to build what is apparently a very big work for the LORD. However, the long term fruitlessness will sometimes not be apparent for decades. Much harm will also be done if a work is not built on a proper foundation. It is crucial that we build according to Scriptural pattern.

The Tasks of Elders and Deacons

The task of elders and deacons is a task of working with people. Elders are under-shepherds of the flock. They reproduce what they are. Therefore, the standards of 1 Timothy 3 are absolutely essential for an elder. This passage has been too easily rationalized and ignored in the American Christian community and sadly many other cultures as well. My own view is that any Ephesians 4:11 leader – whether function or office, whether in the congregation or one with significant ministry influence – should fulfill 1 Timothy 3 standards. There should be a board of leaders for every ministry that affirms a Scriptural call to a ministry. This would clean up much of the mess and scandal. Deacons as well coordinate ministries and work with people. People who do not work well with others are simply unqualified to lead.

This leads to an important axiom: self-appointed leaders. There should be no self-appointed elders in the Body of the Messiah. It should be clear that there is no such thing as a self-appointed elder in Scripture or a democratically elected one, though congregational confirmation is important. However, this is sadly too common today with many disasters following. The damage to naïve people who follow such self-appointed leaders is all too common. Charisma must not supersede character, which is usually the case when such folks seem to succeed. Elders are appointed by other elders or – in the case of pioneer congregations – by elders who function in an apostolic role. We have seen so many unnecessary splits in congregations due to the spirit of independence in our age. A person comes to disagree, and therefore simply goes out and starts their own work and hopes others will follow them out, though there are no moral or theological grounds to justify a split. The leader who splits off appoints himself to the new leadership position. If one is called to plant, one should first find an eldership to whom they are submitted and after proving, be sent and overseen by them.

In Israel, I have painfully seen the principle of local authority violated as those who split congregations gain an appointment by foreign organizations with no real indigenous authority in Israel. I have seen this happen in other countries as well. We are so given to anarchy instead of to the unity for which Yeshua prayed (John 17:21).

It is not as easy as one might think to find people who fulfill leadership standards according to Scripture. Indeed, many are motivated to leadership to boost their ego because the relational base of their life is not solid. It is a law of spiritual life that to the extent that one's relational life is not solid, to that extent the motivations for serving will be off. Ego compensation will be characteristic. It cannot be too strongly emphasized that leadership in the New Covenant order is *servant leadership*. The motive of leadership is love for the LORD and others. Wider servant-hood comes when a person desires to pour their life out in love for the LORD. This style of leadership is to be firm and loving (love and justice go hand in hand in the Scriptures). Leadership is not to provide an occasion for controlling or lording it over others. Non-relational people will have a great deal of trouble with this.

CHAPTER 2

Equipping Leadership

The Model of Ephesians 4

Ephesians 4:11-16 is an important section for understanding the role of leaders. It is recommended that the reader take the time to read it. We read that the Messiah Jesus has given five kinds of leadership roles: apostles, prophets, evangelists, pastors, and teachers. (Some have argued that pastor-teacher is one function and speak of four-fold ministry instead of five-fold. This difference is not significant to what I am expounding here.) These five roles are described as "equipping the saints for the work of service." The implication of the chapter is that each member of the Body is to submit, to be equipped, and to serve consistently in the Kingdom of God. The Body is to be built up by what "every joint supplies." The whole body is to be built together with each member doing "their share." In this structure, the Congregation of Yeshua is to come to maturity, not being blown about by every wind of doctrine. Then we come to the "unity of faith" and to the "stature of the fullness of Messiah" in us.

The key element here is that the gift ministers function in plurality and mutual submission. They give each other space for their proper functioning; they are released by one another. It is possible

9

that one person moves in more than one function, and very rarely a person may function in all five. The LORD, it seems, has rather set things up so there will be an interdependent leadership. As I studied these roles in the Scriptures, I came to the conclusion that they are all expressions of eldership when exercised by men. Some believe that gift-ministers are one step beyond eldership. Women may perform parallel functions on a deacon level. However, eldership gift functions are generally Scripturally reserved for men. We will see this more clearly as we deal with 1 Timothy 3. We will also see that New Covenant authority is always expressed in a plurality of elders in mutual accountability. This plurality functions best with a head elder moderating and leading the plurality to unity. (I will not argue for this point here. Until I do so, please accept for this presentation.) The key to all five functions is to see that they are not primarily to do the work of the ministry but to equip the saints. On the other hand, they equip the saints by being an example of doing what they are training others to do.

The Evangelists

Evangelists eat and sleep with a concern to win the lost to the Kingdom of God. The evangelists should obviously be very capable at personal evangelism. An evangelist's job is also to train the flock to be effective in witness. If there are evangelists at an Ephesians 4 level in the congregation, people should regularly be added to the community because of this witness – and the congregation will become evangelistic by their influence on others. The idea that an evangelist is primarily a person who preaches in evangelistic meetings is a western misunderstanding, though an evangelist may do this. The evangelists can do public preaching. Not all will do this. However, most can learn to effectively lead others to the LORD through their equipping. Evangelists influence the whole flock to share their burden for the lost.

The Pastors

The pastors are primarily oriented to working toward the goal of the sheep being made whole and fulfilling their destiny in the LORD. This includes building others into meaningful relationships (in marriage, family and community). Pastors produce loving congregations. They have a heart of compassion for the sheep, but like good parents, they will also see that discipline and standards are enforced in the congregation. Love motivates their commitment to discipline. When they equip the flock, the members begin to care for one another's needs. The whole congregation becomes pastoral in their heart toward each another.

The Teachers

The teachers are concerned that the flock be well taught in the Scriptures. Unless there is a clear understanding of the Scriptures, the flock will be subject to every wind of doctrine. A teaching motivated elder desires the flock to know the whole Scriptures from Genesis to Revelation. They bear the burden that the whole council of God, on all important subjects, be imparted to the people. They can give themselves to study and teaching for hours on end and experience great joy in being privileged to teach. The effect of the teachers is a well taught flock where most members can teach newcomers the basics of the faith.

The Prophets

The prophets are concerned that righteousness be established in the flock and that the congregation and the individuals within it have a prophetic destiny in their lives. Prophets are gifted with hearing the voice of the LORD more regularly and clearly than other leaders. Supernatural prophetic words confirm directions in the lives of the people and the flock. This includes accurate prophetic dreams, words of knowledge in ministry, and more. However, the truly prophetic people do not just minister in the gift of prophecy, but also in calls to holiness, repentance, and faith that the LORD's Kingdom order might be established.

How accurate does prophetic gifting have to be in the New Covenant? There is some debate on this issue. Generally I give high marks to Wayne Grudem's book *The Gift of Prophecy in the New Testament and Today.* He is a professor at Trinity Evangelical Divinity School in Deerfield, Illinois. My view is an extension of his, as follows. I believe that since the outpouring of the Spirit at Pentecost (Shavuot), every disciple can perceive the word of the Spirit of the LORD. All can be prophetic from time to time. One who is a prophet is one who ministers regularly in prophecy and calls the community to righteousness and faith. However, the need for exacting accuracy all of the time is simply not as it was in the Hebrew Scriptures. We read of no great sanctions in the New Testament against those who miss a prophetic word. All are called to weigh the prophetic word by the Scripture and their sense of confirmation by the Spirit (1 Corinthians 14). One who attains a persistent accuracy and regularity in ministry is recognized in prophetic ministry. However, since the coming of the Spirit, the LORD does not want His people wrongly dependent on prophets. This is an aspect of the New Covenant Age. I do believe that there is potential for the LORD to raise prophets of a different order than we have yet seen. These will be prophets who will speak to nations with great signs and wonders. Revelation 11 describes two last-days prophets who have prophetic ability like Moses and Elijah. Now 100% accuracy is nowhere required in the New Testament for prophetic ministry. Consequently, most people who prophesy should avoid the "thus saith the LORD" type words and simply speak their word for the benefit of the congregation. Some fear that prophetic ministry would detract from the Scriptural prophetic writers. This is a misunderstanding. Prophetic ministry is for confirmation, encouragement, direction and application. It is not for writing revelation. The canon is closed, and it is the foundation for all ministry. Doctrine is built only from the written Scriptures.

The effect of a prophet in a community is to produce a community of people that are prophetic. They seek after the LORD and hear the Spirit's direction for their lives. They are people of destiny.

The Apostles

The last role mentioned is the gift of the apostle. This gift includes the planting and overseeing of congregations. It includes such functions as pastoring pastors, fostering new ministries, and raising up and helping new leaders to get established. We believe that something of the apostolic function has always existed in establishing the Christian community on the foreign mission field and in spurring new movements of congregations. John Wesley is a particularly significant example. This function is an ordinary function just as the other four. Unfortunately, the word "apostle" has become so associated with the function of the 12 and the New Testament writers that many fear to use the word although the New Testament does provide this broader meaning as well. Apostles with a small "a" have a governing function. They are one of the governing elders in a local congregation where they reside. However, they especially are able to tie together the other gift ministers to function in unity. Often gift ministers seek to mold the community after their own gifting. It is important to see that all giftings are released to function. Apostles are especially important in the leadership council of networks of congregations. Five-fold leaders on such a council keep the network from becoming a mere bureaucratic organization, for they continually seek life and growth for the all the congregations of the network.

When a congregation does not have the benefit of all five gift ministries, the leaders need to be willing to draw from the resources of ministries from other congregations and even networks. Indeed, even when the congregation counts ministers with all five gifts in its ranks, it is important to receive outside opinions. This causes freshness and adds new perspective to the community. It is a great factor in growth and maturity.

The Heart of a Servant

Again I want to emphasize the heart of true leaders. It is demonstrated by Yeshua who washed His disciples' feet. The heart of love in the leadership causes them to want to serve the sheep. This is part of the reason for Yeshua teaching us to eschew titles. Of course leadership functions are to be recognized and respected. The people are to respect their leaders since they function as representatives of the LORD in the work of the Spirit. However, the leader does not live for respect. There is no clergy-laity distinction in the Scriptures. Anyone who is called and serves can move into the leadership functions of Ephesians 4. Leadership is broader territory for servanthood. It is the willingness to bear greater responsibility and sacrifice for the Kingdom of God. The greater the love, the greater the scope of authority one has. In our stream of congregations, Tikkun International, we ordain elders and deacons with the laying on of hands. We recognize people in five-fold functions with prophecy, prayer, and the laying on of hands. This recognition of five-fold ministry is fluid since a person may come into new functions and anointing by the Spirit and be recognized again as moving in new equipping roles.

Senior Elder

In most groups there is usually a leader who arises to moderate and aid the group in coming to unity. We believe there is a role of senior elder/leader. In addition, in any group of leaders, one will stand out as simply having a stronger gift of leadership. Before describing the role of senior elder, we must honestly note that the emphasis of the New Testament is not on a senior elder. The emphasis is a plurality of elders.

In the book of Acts, Paul established a plurality of elders. No head pastor is even mentioned. The letters of Paul are addressed to congregations without mentioning a head pastor. Many people point to the following indications for the existence of head pastors: the letters in the Book of Revelation are addressed to messengers. Are these head pastors? What about the pastoral epistles addressed to Titus and Timothy? Some would argue that these are addressed to fellow apostles, not to pastors. Some believe that the messenger over the churches in Revelation 2-3 is the apostolic leader (overseer, bishop) of the congregation of each city that may have numbered in the thousands. However, it should be noted that these messenger leaders were local and seem to have no function outside their own cities. When we speak of senior elders over local congregations, therefore, we are speaking from a practical orientation of what seems to work best, although the Scriptural support for this is limited. In addition, the senior elder may be one functioning in other gift functions while having a pastor in the midst. The leader would just have a stronger gift. However, usually the pastoral gift works best in headship after a planting season. In addition, all elders should have some pastoring ability as part of what eldership is.

A biographical account may be helpful in clarifying my understanding of the role of the senior elder. I was raised through junior and senior high school in the Reformed Church of America. In my mid 20s I was ordained into the Presbyterian Church. My understanding of the pastoral role was naturally formed in this context. I understood the pastor to be the one who did the weekly preaching. This was seen as the most important part of his job. He also gave spiritual counsel and comfort to those in need. It was his job to do funerals, weddings, baptisms, dedications, and to officiate at the serving of the Messiah's Supper. My view was that through a good pastor fulfilling these roles people would be committed to win others to the LORD and to the congregation. In seminary days, I began to question this structure of the local congregation. Perhaps it was a structure that worked in small town parishes and stable neighborhoods of yesteryear. Yet as a young man, I was concerned that many members of the Body were making their decisions concerning where they lived and how they were involved according to economic considerations. The fabric of community was being destroyed by a tyranny of mobility for economic advance. Furthermore, the congregational community was not a primary consideration in decision making. Congregations were joined and then left as easily as one would change clothes. Thus I saw alienation and emptiness in the relational part of people's lives. I came to believe that congregational commitment should be the primary consideration in where to live – that Kingdom of God considerations should be first. After all, Jesus taught, "Seek first His kingdom and His righteousness" (Matthew 6:33). Then the economic realm would fall into place for us.

By the time I graduated from seminary I had been pastoring a congregation for a year. I called upon people to build a community of mutual commitment. The congregants were encouraged to not see the congregation as a place where one goes to a meeting. Scripturally, we do not go to Church, we are the Church. We go to meetings and celebrations of the community. I called for people to buy into accountability, by which they would share their lives with others. This should include letting friends and leaders in on our most significant decisions for prayer, counsel, and discernment. Yes, the final decision must be according to the person's conscience before the LORD. However, the claims of building community and the relational dimensions of life should have more of a claim on us than has been the common practice. We should consider not only the immediate temptation of material progress. To do this, I saw the need for small groups to share and pray together. In Chicago, a community of over forty adults was established who chose to live within walking distance of one another. Most of the other half of the congregation lived within reasonable driving distance.

These basic convictions have stuck during all these 40 plus years in ministry. The senior elder must be one who builds people into the commitment of New Covenant community. I saw that the leader had to establish a counter culture to our self-centered alienated society. The pressures against stable community are still enormous in most western countries, and few congregations build in a way as to overcome these pressures and to create long term community stability. Despite these early convictions I still had much more to learn. In our small Chicago community, I was able to handle the primary pastoral care of the flock. This would change when I accepted a call to lead Beth Messiah Congregation in Washington, D.C.

Beth Messiah was a moderate sized congregation of over 130. There were many hurting people. I offered myself to counsel and pastor the people, but I was totally unprepared for the amount of counsel, demand, strife, and difficulty that such a group could generate. One month we logged over five hundred calls for help. I was overwhelmed, worn out, and losing the support of my abandoned wife. It was at this point that I began to ask other pastors about their lives. Were they happy? How did they handle the pressures? I was amazed at the answers. Actually they were not answers but attempts at evasions. "We will reap a good reward if we do not grow weary in well doing." "The LORD is good." "Yes," I protested, "but I did not ask if the LORD is good, but whether you were happy in the pastoral ministry." I found that most of the pastors I was meeting were unhappy. Their expectations were not fulfilled. They constantly experienced guilt and frustration that they were not meeting the needs of the people. Evangelism was not greatly successful. Even new and larger congregations gained their members from lateral transfer, not from conversions from the lost. Yet, these men were putting in long hours from morning until night over six or seven days a week. Most people have no idea or empathy for what most pastors go through – the long hours, the disappointments, the betrayals, and the attacks. Those whom the pastor seeks to help often turn on them and blame them for their problems when they are not helped. Pastors enter the ministry in idealism. Many are caring and sensitive people who desire to truly love and care for the sheep. The model they are following sets them up for burn out or disillusionment: "Perhaps we cannot accomplish that much after all." Their salaries are often too little to raise a family and send the children to college! Poverty is considered good for the pastor.

In my own beginning symptoms of burn out, the LORD graciously led me to a meeting of Christian leaders and wives in our area. This was a group of charismatic pastors from several streams who claimed to believe in the restoration of the last days Church to unity, power, Holy Spirit gifting, and the establishment of the roles of five-fold ministry. This was a new idea to me. I later became convinced that Scripture supported this theology (especially John 17 and Ephesians 4-5). It was believed by the Puritans and by many leaders of the historic revivals.

One pastor stood out to me in this group as he shared some very basic concepts he had learned. His name was Pierre Bynum. Pierre was not seminary trained but seemed to think clearly. I asked him my persisting question. "Are you happy in the ministry?"

"Of course, aren't you?" he said.

I responded, "I mean … how do you find time to meet the needs of the people with counseling, the administration, and the teaching? Do you have time for your family?"

His response amazed and intrigued me. He said, "I perceive that your problem is that you have bought into the traditional pastoral role."

"What's that?" I responded.

Pierre and I made an appointment to get together, with our spouses included, to talk about this problem. Patty and I also met with a dear elder friend and colleague, Michael Rudolph, who put a scheduling limit on my pastoral involvement. He required that I spend family time for two hours most days and have a full day off. Mike and I have now walked together for over 40 years.

Amazingly, during this period, *Time Magazine* came out with an article on why pastors burn out. Some commit suicide and far too many were ending up in mental hospitals. Why? Time concluded that this could be traced to the following factors. Pastors are usually sensitive people who have a nebulous and impossible job description. They are charged to be excellent teachers, counselors, and to be available for calls. Pastors are expected to meet the needs of parishioners, to do the weddings, funerals, and marriage counseling. Community involvement is a must. Sociologists estimated that accomplishing these tasks could very well take 120 to 180 hours a week. Because all this is expected, the pastor must neglect his family. Most of what he does disappoints him because of its lack of excellence. Yet this excellence is impossible because of the large amount of "stuff" to be done. Furthermore, many pastors have not yet been delivered from perfectionism. The sociologists and psychologists at *Time* concluded that a wholly different job description needed to be developed.

Our evening with the Bynums was one of the most momentous of our lives. Pierre laid out his schedule and the nature of his vision of the role of the head pastor. Before giving a modified outline of my present understanding of what I learned from Pierre, I want to say the following. First, many will not want to take the route being recommended here. The reason is that the traditional role provides gratifications for both the pastor and the people. The pastor gets the status of being the only one in the community that can do the quasi-mystical tasks of the traditional role. People can become spectators who are required to give little beyond attendance and funds. Actually, the most successful traditional churches rarely have more than 15% of their membership in active committed service (see Ralph Neighbor's book *Where Do We Go From Here?*). This is an unholy deal that far too many are willing to make.

The Scriptural role for the pastor begins with the understanding that he is only one of the gift-ministry leaders. Together they are to equip the saints to do the work of the ministry. The primary function of the leadership is to equip and to train others in ministry functions. Of course discipleship and counsel are part of this training that all may attain to their calling and to the pattern of life enjoined in the New Covenant. However, when the flock progresses beyond 25 people, one person cannot adequately do it all. Research on church growth suggests that fifteen families are the very maximum for pastoral care. Beyond community building and pastoral care are the Scriptural ideals of an evangelistic people who are prophetic and well taught in the Scriptures!

How therefore does a pastor spend his time? Primarily in the raising up of leaders! It is in developing a leadership core who will share the work of shepherding the flock and equipping all of the saints to do the work of the ministry. This ministry is to take place both in the congregation and in the world of the lost. After following this model for 30 years, not only has it been proven to work, but several other congregations have been birthed from home group structures from the mother congregation. Leaders have been trained within and sent forth to plant new works.

It was a humbling but wonderful experience to listen to Pierre. Here was a man trained in the structure of charismatic churches teaching me, the seminary graduate, how to be a pastor.

Time Management

What does the head pastor's role consist of? His most important task is to minister to his family and be a good husband and father. Furthermore, since much ministry is to couples, it is the ideal that the wife would work with him in ministry. Ministry can then draw them together instead of separating them. For this to take place the pastor (and other gift-ministers as well) needs to block out daily time for family, days off, vacation time, and special time away with his wife. Learning the skills of prayerful calendar planning and coordination with his wife and leadership team are crucial if the pastor is not to become merely a responder to circumstances. Wrong priorities are a pitfall to avoid, according to Charles Hummel's famous phrase "being under the tyranny of the urgent." With few exceptions, I suggest two hours a day at least five days a week – including dinner – plus one solid day off. During these periods the concentration is on family members. Other friends can be invited to participate. However, the time is not for congregational concerns. In addition to Charles Hummel, I want to mention Stephen Covey and his *Seven Habits of Highly Effective People*. Effective leaders are not to live under the tyranny of the urgent, only responding to circumstances. They live in one of four quadrants which Covey names as important, but not urgent. This is where we are proactive, and most of the particularly important work is done. Yes, there is the important and urgent. There is a death, a medical emergency, a fire, or other events that require our full effort. But many mistake unimportant things as important and give themselves to the quadrant Covey calls urgent and unimportant. Everyone can be idle or can procrastinate. This is the not important and not urgent quadrant. However, everyone needs down time to chill out, so maybe some things in this quadrant are important. The baseball game or the movie can be important if they are not dominant involvements. Covey's book is highly recommended.

Time with Potential Leaders

The second thing that needs to be planned is time to meet with potential leaders. These should be chosen according to who is closest to fulfilling 1 Timothy 3 standards for elders or deacons. They then are trained and discipled to fully meet the standards for these roles. Two evenings a week can be given over to raising leaders on a couple to couple basis. The head pastor may meet with two couples, or a couple and a single, called to leadership. In this informal context there is a time of vision raising, prayer, and sharing on leadership principles. Friendship and loyalty are built at these times. *There should at least be an evening a month for leadership training in a larger group context too.* Furthermore, there can be whole days or weekends together. We have done this twice a year. When the congregation is small, the leader/head pastor should do some counseling, but this will be transferred as leaders are raised up.

The Home Cell Group

The key foundation in our model of building is the home group structure. When a congregation is first being planted, the senior elder leads the home group. However, his goal is to raise two leaders out of the home group and to see the original group become two. He will then visit the home groups but not lead one. He will instead give himself to the home group leaders. The home group is the building block of community life, for this is the place for shared spiritual life in the power of the Holy Spirit. The central services are celebrations of a community, based on the home group structure. When we deal with this structure, we understand that a choice must be made. Is a congregation to be understood as shared life in community or a meeting-rally where people go to hear a sermon, good music, and to worship? We do not believe that the latter makes up a Scriptural congregation. Gathering to worship and hear the Scriptures taught is a significant function of a congregation. It fulfills a priestly duty of worship and intercession which preserves the world until the Messiah comes, parallel to Jewish thinking about the Synagogue and the House of Study. However, central programs do not produce New Testament life! The presence and ministry of the Holy Spirit in a personal context is the *sine qua non* of New Covenant life. This occurs when every person is engaged in ministering and receiving through the gifts of the Spirit. This can only happen effectively in small groups. The kind of meeting described in 1 Corinthians 14, where all can minister in the gifts of the Spirit in one gathering, is obviously a home meeting.

It is good in the early life of the congregation to expose the community to the ministry of other gift-ministers who can aid in vision and equipping. Small congregations do not have five-fold ministry present in their midst. All five are needed. Therefore the senior elder needs to be secure enough to see others used. Planting is hard if not done by either 1) a person who combines the gifts of pastor and evangelist as giftings, or 2) two people with each gift that plant together, or 3) an apostle. A pastor will often plant and build by lateral transfer because his pastoral or teaching gift draws disciples, but this has little effect on the lost and does not really extend the Kingdom.

Expect Opposition

The reader should note that switching from a functioning traditional model to an equipping model will not be received without opposition. At Beth Messiah these comments were heard: "If you are going to use lay people to shepherd the congregation, then what are we paying you do?" "Now there is a two tiered membership. There is the 'in membership' that can come to the leadership meetings – and the rest of us." However, when the sheep find that the new orientation provides more intimacy and fulfillment, many will switch their loyalty to the new model. Still, many are not looking for intimacy. They are looking for a good show once a week. At Beth Messiah, therefore, membership was through home group commitment and not by merely attending the weekly celebration.

Elders

The role of eldership is foundational for all of the five-fold gift ministries of Ephesians 4. In my view every gift-ministry person needs to attain a basic ability of shepherding even if his primary calling will not be as a pastor. Growing in love and care for people is a key to other roles being exercised in balance. All gift ministry men should be true elders. Women who express significant Ephesians 4 ministry gifts should be deacons.

In our view, the Scripture is most clear in 1 Timothy 3 and Titus 1 that governmental authority is given to men who prove headship in families. To hear from the LORD, to set direction, to enforce standards, to love, to show hospitality, and to judge fairly with wise judgment are crucial functions of elders. In regard to male eldership, we note with regard to the women having equal opportunity to governing eldership, that this creates the strange situation of the husband, as the head of his home, submitting to his wife as pastor. Rather than the elder just being a talking head, he is to be one who reproduces family health and order in the congregation. Can there be exceptional single elders, and even women sometimes? Yes, but generally, the standard is that men are chosen on the basis of their family life as one of the key criteria. There are other criteria too.

The elder should be one that has an exemplary family life and fulfills the standards of 1 Timothy 3 and Titus 1. All should read these passages prayerfully. I used to think that elders expressed their ministry through leading the cell groups, and that one needed to be an elder to lead one. I now believe requiring people to attain eldership level before leading cell groups restricts growth. Rather an elder is one who oversees several cell groups and is able to shepherd the leaders of these groups. To do this, the potential elder is proven concerning counseling, small group teaching, and in lovingly enforcing standards in his family and his home group leadership.

An elder is one who has a quality devotional life and can convey the life of the LORD to others. He is involved in a very full way with Kingdom concerns: helping to raise new leaders, overseeing ministries, and sharing the good news with the lost.

The elder will sit on the governing council of the congregation. I recommend that this council meet at least once a month. We do relieve some elders who have special callings from this responsibility. As part of this council, he must make decisions concerning congregational discipline. He sits therefore as a member of the court of the congregation. In this function as a judge, he must be trained in making decisions based on an adequate presentation of the evidence. It is crucial to understand the judicial function of the elders, and I strongly recommend my book *Due Process* in this regard. Many congregations simply do not have functioning elderships that meet regularly, oversee the total work of the congregation, and handle disputes with loving discipline. It is crucial to establish this.

The Spouse is Needed

A true elder is one who has brought his wife to share in the concerns of the Kingdom. Much of the work of the elder is really the work of an eldership couple ministering to other couples. The importance of this becomes even more significant when we see the inappropriateness of men ministering to women in counseling situations. Indeed, counseling is an intimate exchange. The bonding that takes place in this exchange is becoming well known. At Beth Messiah, men were not to counsel women in a one-on-one relationship. Elders among women, who are either deacons in their own right or wise elders' wives, are to take on this role of counseling women. The counseling needs of members are to be met first by wise members of the Body, and only when necessary by elders. Although it is good to provide many capable counselors in a growing community, training the members to love and care for one another will cut down on the counseling load. Training in basic counseling was a staple of our congregational life.

Deacons

Deacons (Hebrew *shamashim*) have usually been understood as those who oversee administrative functions in the congregation to relieve elders for teaching and other ministering. As such, deacons must also attain an ability to work with people and to govern in their administrative fields. Whether in education supervisors, bookstore overseers, overseers of the distribution of clothes and food to the poor, or audio ministry coordinators, deacons must be able to enforce standards of responsibility for all who are in the ministry with them. The Scriptures in Acts 6 and 1 Timothy 3 make it clear that deacons are not just those who serve (the literal meaning of the term) but are those who administrate serving areas. Therefore, the standards for deacons are similar to the requirements for elders. The difference is in teaching and shepherding ability. The record of the book of Acts shows that the first deacons were men of extraordinary quality. I believe that Scripture allows for women deacons. Dale Rumble of Fountain of Life Church has written excellent material on the importance of deacons. Elders oversee deacons in their work. Some teach that all elders should first be proven at a deacon level.

Many deacons can shepherd. For them, deacon level responsibility will be expressed in caring for people and perhaps eventual eldership. Others will not be oriented to personally care for people in this way. Therefore we have concluded that there are shepherding deacons and administrative deacons. It is important to recognize that the gifts of some will not fit them for shepherding roles. Other roles are important to the life of the congregation, and therefore we must not seek to squeeze everyone into the same role.

Raising up Leaders

The primary focus of head leaders is to raise new leaders. Only when this is the focus can the Kingdom expand. The LORD's rule or

Kingdom is through those who are established in mature leadership. A community can truly make disciples only to the extent that they raise leaders to disciple others and to foster home groups. In these home groups, true spiritual intimacy and bonding take place when the Holy Spirit is present and the use of spiritual gifts is encouraged. Preaching at the larger celebration of the congregation is important if the Scriptures is well taught, but this is inadequate in making disciples. Disciples are made when a leader says, "Watch what I do." After this, the disciple is told to do the work while the discipler watches. This pattern in discipling is the key to training others to be witnesses, to move in the power of the Holy Spirit, to disciple new members of the Body, to lead small groups, and to administrate areas of congregational life.

The leader of the newly formed small congregation must choose those with whom he will intensively work. First, they are those who are worshipers of the LORD. They truly give themselves in corporate worship participation and in private devotional life. Second, they are those who have a teachable spirit. They can humbly receive correction while being trained. Third, they have their family life in order – a true love relationship with their wives. Their children obey them and standards of Scriptural behavior are enforced in the home. By the way, we are not to expect perfect robotic behavior for children. The issue is that children are ultimately submitted and regularly brought into line as they are growing up. Lastly they show responsibility in serving, including follow through, the meeting of deadlines, and the producing of quality work.

Obviously no one should be in head leadership who does not fulfill these standards! Yet, sadly, we have many leaders in the Body today who do not fulfill Scriptural requirements. I truly believe that it would be better if these leaders would step out of leadership and send their followers to congregations where Scriptural standards are fulfilled. These are not the only standards for leaders, but the ones I listed form a good foundation for those who are to be raised into leadership. One person worried that requiring these standards would shut down half the congregations in the western world. Yet, if all were submitted to the other half, they would soon reproduce health and growth to make up for the deficit. Remember, we reproduce what we are, not just what we say.

Capability in leadership is also crucial! Ineffective leaders thwart the potential of many disciples. If our sloppy standards were the rule in the business world, our society would be in poverty! Today's society is in such a mess that many leaders will say that they do not see anyone who fulfills the criteria to be in leadership training. The solution to this is simple. We pick a few couples and singles who are the closest to fulfilling these criteria and disciple them so that they do fulfill the criteria. We work with them intensively in these four areas!

The Congregational Structure for Kingdom Expansion

The measure for success is twofold: outreach to the lost and discipleship of members of the Body to live out a Kingdom life! Most congregations' leadership agrees with this simple statement. It is not the number of attendees at a meeting, which may have little significance to the LORD. Americans are enamored of numbers, and we have given in to a false value structure from the world! The LORD is very little concerned, as I see Scripture, whether a congregation is large or small. Whether the structure is one congregation of five thousand members, or one hundred congregations of fifty members, the quality of outreach and discipleship is our gauge. The LORD's concern is the quality of life among the people. The LORD is not concerned with the numbers a leader can brag about, especially since some people go where the entertainment is the best. Rather He is concerned with the masses coming to know Him and then becoming disciples. The LORD could little care whether there are 10,000 meeting under one institutional umbrella called a congregation, as compared to 100 congregations of 100. If the

Kingdom is extended, people are made into effective disciples, true community is established, the majority of the members are engaged in Kingdom work, and the lost are being won – this is a successful congregation, whether it is 100 or 10,000.

In Illinois, Bill Hybels built one of the most famous mega-churches and led the movement toward seeker friendly services. He recently confessed shock at the fact that most of his members were not discipled. Others have raised the issue of the ineffectiveness in discipleship of today's church models. Dallas Willard, in his monumental book *The Divine Conspiracy*, is one of the great inspirational reads with concrete direction for discipleship. Per Willard, a disciple is one who obeys all the commands of Yeshua since this was His Word to His apostles in commanding them to disciple the nations in Matthew 28:20 (NIV) – *"Teaching them to obey everything that I have commanded you."* The basic curriculum of discipleship is the commandments of Yeshua. It is a very comprehensive course. Yet in many of these mega-church congregations, intimacy and discipleship have a lot of room for growth. What is happening in these institutions? Usually these elements are present: a very entertaining speaker, an upbeat music program, low demand projections from the pulpit (just attend, tithe, and live by the Scriptures for successful life), the comfort that all is well, and heaven is assured. These mega-churches fit our modern mobility and consumerism, which is self-oriented. The Scriptures are not to become our means of achieving our true goals of personal peace and affluence.

Thankfully there have been some changes since the first edition of this book. A 1992 article in *Christianity Today* documented a significant fact. Most of the mega-churches in America with thousands of members then were built by lateral transfer, as 95% of the members simply moved to the new mega-church from other congregations. There was very little evangelistic impact. The article's author noted that these mega-churches were simply parallel to the new supermarkets that put the local "mom and pop" stores out of business. Thankfully this percentage has increased, per 2014 research as reported in *Charisma Magazine.* Today nearly 25% of mega-church members had not been in any church for a long time before coming to a megachurch.[1] This is a noteworthy shift.

In 1990, Ralph Neighbor documented the following in his monumental book *Where Do We Go from Here?* In such institutions (I avoid calling them congregations by Scriptural norms), only 5-15% of the people were involved in service and witness. The rest were mere attendees. Neighbor also shows that there are mega-churches built on the right model of evangelism and discipleship. Some of them number in the tens of thousands. Thankfully mega-churches are moving in the right direction, as reported in the same *Charisma* article mentioned previously. Research now shows that 55% of megachurch attendees volunteer at the church in some way, which is a higher percentage than in smaller churches. These are significant changes.

Lest the reader misunderstand, I am not against big congregations. If a big meeting attracts the lost because there is an excellent speaker and good music ... great! However, by the evidence of good science, these congregations were having little effect on the lost. Thankfully this seems to be changing. But at worst, they were offering shallow messages to their existing disciples. Has this changed? Of course, the pastor preaching to 100 can more easily speak at a deeper level.

The issue of what institutional framework to produce (large congregations or several smaller ones) is largely a question of the leading of the Spirit. The head leader needs to make sure his pride does not cause mishearing. Some have multiplied many small congregations, and others have given leadership to what has become a mega-church. There are different kinds of leadership callings and giftings. There are different styles of congregational life that will draw different kinds of people!

For the last 30 years, Beth Messiah Congregation and then its plantings have followed the cell model put forth here. By the standards of many other congregations, we have done well. By the

LORD's standards we have far to go. Thankfully, many mega-churches offer small groups now. We have seen our model of a cell congregation accomplish the following things. First, we were a mother congregation of 350-400 people who were organized into cell structures. This congregation had a majority of people who were either first baptized in our midst or have made their first quality commitment to congregational life in our midst. Scores of people have been baptized at Beth Messiah Congregation. Beth Messiah spurred several congregations locally and in other geographic locations. The standards of the LORD are part of this discipleship. Over the last 30 years we have seen very little in divorces or family break up in any of our congregations. Those few who have been divorced in our midst occurred either when the pagan spouse abandoned the marriage or due to exceptional falls into temptation. Where couples made a quality commitment to the Kingdom, there has been no divorce. Many whose marriages were very difficult have been healed. This is the case with over a thousand people in families connected to our congregations. This is the product of an intimate support structure mediating the grace of the LORD. In recent years, George Barna has shown through massive research surveys that the great bulk of professing members of the Body are not discipled. Yet the cell model provides a place of intimate discipleship.

The fact that our congregations were formed to impact the Jewish community makes this a more significant accomplishment. We have chosen to multiply congregations locally and abroad. Three planting families have been sent to Israel and two planting families have been sent to Russia. In addition, many support emissaries have been sent. At one period, over forty families and individuals were sent overseas due to the opportunities of harvest.

I want to make it absolutely clear that this success is not because of any great talent or natural charisma among our leaders. Most of us see ourselves as ordinary people who have been able by the grace of the LORD to maintain a covenant commitment to each other over the years. We have worked hard and by the grace of the LORD have been given some success. From our multiplication, a full time school named Messiah Biblical Institute was formed. This school today functions as Messianic Life Institute under Mike Rudolph. Messiah Biblical Institute was one of the catalysts of forming Messianic Jewish Bible Institutes that have provide training in Ukraine, Russia, Brazil, Argentina, Israel, and Ethiopia. The school also served other churches in our area. Ets Chaiyim School was a full time K-8 school, and a cooperative high school that functioned for ten years was also birthed. Lastly, in its beginning years, we gave leadership and financial support toward the success of a national association of Messianic Jewish congregations, the Union of Messianic Jewish Congregations (UMJC).

Where then has our weakness been? I believe that it has been in moving our cell group structure toward truly effective evangelism, which is different than reaching unchurched Christians. As part of this, some of our cell groups have become too large and have duplicated our Saturday services with worship and teaching. We discourage this. Group meetings need to be interactive and emphasize sharing and mutual prayer and support. Every cell group is more effective when it is small; Neighbor says less than sixteen. Every group needs to emphasize evangelism and discipleship. To do this, our understanding of qualifications for cell group leadership needs to be adjusted, and our understanding of the pattern of discipleship needs to be improved. However, this is hard to do in our culture.

The Neighbor Model of Cell Groups

It is my nature to seek the universal principle, but then adjust it to specific circumstances. In this regard, I am convinced that the writings of Ralph Neighbor capture a key dimension of the restoration of the Body. Neighbor's basic book is *Where Do We Go From Here?* Neighbor has also developed much in the way of resources for the cell based congregation. However, this material will need to be revised for those who lead Messianic Jewish congregations. Beth Messiah Congregation simplified and adapted this program for Messianic Jewish congregations. Although I believe that Neighbor discovered universal truth about how the congregation of Yeshua is to operate in every culture, I do not believe that every detail of Neighbor's program is universally helpful. Neighbor argues for the following:

1) *There are two basic models for congregational life.* One is the program based design, and the other is the cell based design. The first is an un-Scriptural shadow of congregational life. Central programs and meetings are foundational in this model. Those given to this model are ineffective in penetrating the world of the lost. Few members are truly involved in serving (5-15%). They lead Sunday school (Sabbath school), visitation programs, children's clubs, and youth groups. Most are not intimately involved with others, do not minister in the gifts of the Spirit, and are not living a life of prayer. This is even in those congregations that claim to believe in the gifts of the Spirit. Little in the way of gift practice takes place. In the cell based structure, the foundational building block is the small group that meets in homes. In this context, discipleship, intimacy, and the flow of the gifts of the Spirit are normal. Training in evangelism and effective outreach is part of the life of the congregation. Over 90% are involved. The lost are truly being won to the Kingdom.

2) *The cell based model must be sustained by a life of prayer that permeates the lives of the cells, the individual members, and the congregation as a whole.* This level of sustained prayer life is hardly known in the West.

3) *A Scriptural cell congregation must not be confused with the discipleship cell model that became popular in America.* This model did provide intimacy but became an ingrown

community. The goal of evangelism must be truly uppermost in the life of cells. Without this, discipleship is very limited. Healing and intimacy take place in a Kingdom context where all become effective witnesses through the power of the Spirit.

4) *The cell based congregation is not merely one model among others, but is a reflection of the LORD's intended congregational order as seen in the book of Acts.* Here we read how the disciples met from house to house, though they numbered in the thousands. This is proven as well by the most effective congregations in a multitude of cultures and nations. Neighbor has traveled worldwide to study this.

5) *It is very difficult to change a program based design congregation to a cell based design because of the hold of traditional patterns and expectations among people.* It is crucial that all understand and support the cell based design in every cell based congregation. Neighbor is the first I know to fully document and explain the organizational structure of the larger cell based congregations in various cultures. He amazingly finds that most evolved into the same basic structure. I do want to note that I have known several congregations that have transitioned.

There are a few very important developments since Neighbor's work. In South America a new model called G-12 has taken hold. It has been a very effective model. It is summarized in the book *Groups of 12* by Joel Comiskey. G-12 congregations are also based on the small group model. However, they find that two needs are in conflict. One is the long term relational need of the people and the other to evangelize. They find that dividing cell groups tend to disrupt the intimacy of relationships and are resisted by people. Therefore their model is to plant new groups. Each member is part of two groups at all times, one is a group for long term relationships and the other an evangelistic plant which will eventually become the long term relational group. The new group will be made of new people with a leader who still is part of his old group. They actually are therefore part of two small group meetings a week. I do not know of anyone that has accomplished this in the Northern Hemisphere. In such context, modifications have taken place where people meet every other week in each kind of group. Comiskey's book is worth reading.

Larry Kreider with the Dove Network in the United States has been very effective in maintaining a network of congregations firmly based on small group models. Larry has embraced cell group models and G-12 models and is open to whichever a congregation desires. He has also embraced house congregations where the group meeting in the house is the only major commitment to the members of the house congregation. However, he wisely notes that house congregations need to be under a genuine eldership oversight, over several house groups, since such groups are unlikely to have sufficient elders within. In addition, he teaches that they need to be submitted to a five-fold network of congregations for apostolic oversight and equipping. The last I knew, Larry was overseeing some 1,000 people in house congregations as well. In Israel, some of us think that this model may be a helpful supplement to our more traditional congregational models. For one thing it will enable people in the working world to lead them. It will deliver us from the need for finding larger facilities and for raising overseas funds. It could help us to penetrate the larger community. However, I do very strongly endorse Larry's standards for such groups. There must always be a real eldership.

The home group based model for congregations is in my mind a universal Scriptural principle, not just one method among others. I have seen it work in America, Israel, Ukraine, Brazil, and Argentina. However, it requires a pastoral or five-fold leadership that constantly stress its importance and are committed to training leaders to succeed in this foundational orientation. Our monthly leadership training meeting was a key to the success of the small groups.

CHAPTER 3

The Structure of the Congregation

I here summarize for you the structure of congregational life at Beth Messiah Congregation with the revisions we implemented from Neighbor's writings.

The Building Bock: The Chavurah Home Cell Group

The cell group (*chavurah*-fellowship) structure is amazingly capable of providing so very much that otherwise requires a great deal of programming in traditional congregations. The cell is the first level for providing fellowship, training in the gifts of the Spirit, evangelism training, and fellowship gatherings. Cell members try to meet the financial crises of other cell members (with an appeal to the larger congregation for what cannot be met by the small group). Many administrative functions for the larger congregation are handled at this level. Nursery duty at central meetings can be rotated among the established cells as can setup crews, work crews, etc. Ministries to the poor can also be cell based.

We must first look at the cell to see why it is the basic building block for discipling and expanding leadership. The cell leader works with an associate leader (intern). Over time, the cell leader will turn more and more of the leadership of the cell meeting to the associate. The cell leader meets with the associate and evaluates his leadership in group dynamics skills. He must know how to encourage all to share, to operate in the gifts of the Holy Spirit, and to oversee so that no one dominates the group. Therefore, the cell group is the laboratory of leadership training.

In addition, the cell members are discipled in the basic teachings of the congregation by meeting with other cell members who have been through the basic membership course. At Beth Messiah we used *Growing to Maturity*, originally published by the Union of Messianic Jewish Congregations, as well as in its new edition today by Lederer-Messianic Jewish Publications. This can be done on an individual basis, small subgroups of the cell, or in a supporting membership class supplemented by personal meetings with the disciple. Prayer for healing and other needs are also part of the supportive structure of the cell.

Whether by taking out teams in evangelism, discipling new members of the Body, or in leading the groups, the pattern is always to set an example by "doing" and then observing and helping others to grow in their abilities. In addition, real accountability is fostered where members share their struggles. We think of the John Wesley groups where all in the group were to be updated on the questions of victory over sin, depth of devotional life, and witness to the lost. Of course, very sensitive things can only be shared with the leader in private, but there should be an open life before one another.

Connecting to Cells of Lost People

The key to evangelism is seeing that the members of the cell group are integrated into the structures of the lives of the lost. This means encouraging members to join classes, for example, book discussion groups, bowling leagues, or to visit in hotel and restaurant lounges (drink a virgin drink!) where the lost meet. The lost are in cells that are like extended households which Neighbor calls *oikos*.

It is helpful for members of the Body to join these groups in teams. Neighbor even suggests a model of small groups geared for the lost called share groups. These are subgroups of cell groups made up of two-thirds lost people and one-third members of the Body. These groups provide open discussions between members of the Body and the lost without either group dominating. The life of the Spirit provides a non-threatening witness which is effective by the power of the Spirit.

Prayer Meetings

The cell structure is supplemented by regular prayer meetings both of the cell and the central congregation. These prayer meetings are sometimes "all-nighters." There can also be geographically convenient early-morning prayer meetings. Some meetings may be scheduled for daily prayer, and some may be scheduled less frequently. Covering the evangelism and the work of the congregation in sustained regular prayer is very important.

Praying together effectively is difficult for Americans to pull off. So many have their own ideas of how a prayer meeting should be conducted. There is great temptation for spiritual pride and criticism in prayer meetings. In my experience, the best corporate prayer meetings follow a simple structure. A topic is announced by the leadership for prayer. Those present spend time holding this topic up before the LORD in prayer, out loud, and quietly to themselves. All know that everyone present is praying on this subject. After a season of prayer, the leader asks for those who are led to pray out loud in the group, while the rest say amen in agreement to every Scripturally correct prayer. This is a model I have found working effectively in many other parts of the world.

It is important that the leaders set the direction for prayer and decide when to end a season of praying on a specific topic. When others give direction for the prayer meeting through their praying, or seek to question the leader's decision to end a season of prayer for a particular topic (i.e., "The Spirit is telling me we have not broken through yet."), then disunity results. Some will affirm the leader; others will affirm the one with the out of order directional suggestions. In this disunity, power in corporate prayer will be lost. My visits to other nations, where strong corporate prayer meetings are normal life patterns, have convinced me of the importance of submission to leadership for direction in prayer meetings. The leaders that are not chosen to lead the meeting can make private suggestions and even seek the LORD together while others privately pray. However, what is put forth to the meeting must be a clear and singular direction.

Supplementing the Training of the Cell leaders

The cell leader is backed up by the pastor over a group of cells – and ultimately by the head pastor. When situations are too difficult for him, these supportive leaders can be brought in to help. In this model, most of the counseling, discipleship, and evangelism take place on the cell level. The pastor or elder supports the cell leader by not doing counseling unless the cell leader requests it. Cell leaders are trained to know when to request help. He is present when the leader counsels his group members so he can grow in ability. He can probably handle a more difficult case in the future.

The material available to convey in leadership meetings is unlimited if the head pastor is constantly reading and growing. A good leader can gain new insights into deliverance, spiritual life, administration, and more if he is willing to always be a student himself. A leader will never lack for "food" to feed the sheep if he is ever praying, reading, growing, improving, and embracing the truth.

The congregation can provide the supportive training that the cell cannot provide. There were leadership training retreats for cell leaders and associates twice a year at Beth Messiah. In addition, there was a monthly evening meeting given to leadership training and sharing. Furthermore, there were training times for administrative deacons that are not in the cell leadership path: for children's educators, tape ministry coordinators, and other deacons.

It is important that leaders be trained in the knowledge of the Scriptures. Saturday services and preaching provide some of this, as do recommended books. However, the congregation should offer courses on Scriptural theology, counseling, deliverance, ministering healing, marriage and family, and more. We have the advantage of Messiah Life Institute[2] offering many resources via DVD and online media that can now be used as part of training. Messianic Jewish Bible Institute also offers excellent online resources.[3]

An Outline of These Training Areas

1) *Scriptural knowledge is crucial.* The cell leader should know the content of the Scriptures; a basic summary of each of the sixty-six books of the Scriptures.

2) *The basics of theology and ethics should be taught.* They should especially know the meaning of acting in covenant loyalty and the importance of training the flock in this. Our resources for this are *Growing to Maturity*, Keith (Asher) Intrater's *Covenant Relationships*, and my *Due Process*. Until we train up a leadership and a flock that are willing to support Scriptural discipline in the congregation (and inter-congregationally and organizationally), we will be weak targets for the enemy.

3) *How to lead a cell group is, of course, central.* Neighbor's book, *The Shepherd's Guidebook*, is the best I have found to date. Beth Messiah's book, *A Cell Based Congregation*, is a helpful

Messianic Jewish adaptation. The cell leader must be able to challenge and inspire his members to fully commit to the Kingdom of God. Larry Kreider's resources available from Dove in Lancaster, Pennsylvania are also very good.

4) *Training in Scriptural counseling is crucial as well.* We have found that Jay Adams' material (*Christian Counselors Manual*) is helpful for most; however, there are limitations. There is a dogmatic tone and a rejection of the fact that some insights from psychology and psychiatry can be helpful. Furthermore the supernatural power of inner healing and deliverance is missed. I am not talking about some way-out guided imagery trip, but the touch of the power of the cross and the name of Jesus applied to the areas where people are hurting and healing is needed. The writings of Mark Bubeck (*The Adversary*) are helpful. Leanne Payne's *The Healing Presence* is an excellent resource. Of course the ones being trained training to counsel should observe counseling first, and then be observed counseling by the one who trained them. Our counseling is applying the Scriptures to people's lives. It should be understood that we are not training psychologists! John and Paul Sanford's *Transformation of the Inner Man* is very profitable. There are some sections of the book that do need some theological improvement, but the general thrust and information is invaluable. The value of Adams' work is that it helps shepherds avoid being used by those who merely want attention but do not want to change. Establishing a pattern of assignments, to prove the seriousness of the counselees, is very helpful. So is setting a limit for the number of sessions to be given in counseling. The materials of Gary Collins, James Dobson (on child rearing and family life), Larry Christianson, and others are also helpful. We have found that training people to believe that the LORD works through an anointed order is crucial. They embrace the idea that the LORD's help is supernatural.

Their situation does not normally require the help of the head pastor! We also recommend the course in healing counseling by the organization Restoring the Foundations. Additionally, Ellel Ministries, based in England, has excellent training courses. I recommend looking these up on the internet and using them in training leaders.

5) *Training in time-management and administration.* Every cell leader needs to know how to keep a calendar for appointments and to use a calendar to plan his time well. We tell our leaders that most evenings from seven thirty or eight to ten will be given to the Kingdom. Family time should be planned around dinner (two hours) and on the days off. There will be little time for frivolous activities in the life of an effective servant of the Kingdom. However, the Spirit will lead us into times of fun – from tennis, to skiing, to family sports. The pattern of life is reaching out to the lost and discipling new members of the Body. Quality family time will not suffer if the time is given to the family in the early evening hour and during at least part of the day off. Also, the children can be taught that they are part of the "ministry team" and that the LORD can use them to show love. Successful congregations have been able to motivate their people by the Spirit to embrace a sacrificial lifestyle. This is something most Americans instinctively avoid. Most are seeking to withdraw from engagement after their work day or work week is over. This pattern must be broken. Our time is the LORD's time. Cell leaders need also be trained to keep lists of delegated tasks, completion goals, and completed task records. They must establish a regular time to follow up with those who have received delegated tasks and to train them in responsibility. It is often easier to do the task oneself than to delegate. However, this is shortsighted. Eventually the Kingdom will suffer if the

leader follows this pattern because people will not be trained to be responsible.

Families in Ministry

We affirm the idea that husbands and wives ideally minister together. Some have gifts that may require that they also have separate involvements. This is common. However, when they minister as a team in hospitality, counseling, coordination, and service, they can often find great joy in seeing the Spirit use them as a team.

Indeed, whole families can be used as a team. Hospitality can be given to new families whereby the children are trained to welcome and share with the new children. If the whole family is sent home from an enjoyable evening, with even the children speaking positively about the visit, it can greatly aid in building the community.

It is sometimes hard to convince wives that ministering with their husbands is very important. Joint ministry becomes more serious when the husband enters cell group or eldership levels of leadership. If she is a leader in her own sphere, we can rejoice. However, some spouses would rather just be homebodies, raise the children, and leave pastoral ministry to the husband. We have seen men with a real ministry call truly frustrated because of the unwillingness of the wife to minister and to be involved with him. Usually this stems from insecurity on her part. She reasons, "What do I have to add to the conversation or ministry situation?" Unfortunately, if this pattern is not broken, it could lead to ministry pulling them apart rather than drawing them together. She will see the ministry taking him away from her; his time and energies will be given outside the home. Yet if they see the Spirit using them together, they can be drawn into a closer bond through ministry involvement. The woman in this situation will need encouragement to see her worth in the LORD, and that she has unique gifts to give to the Kingdom. She needs to see that her husband needs her by his side.

Another danger for the husband who is involved in ministry without his wife being an active partner with him is the formation of unhealthy soul-ties with other women who are more "dynamic" and "spiritual" than his wife. A wife needs to understand that her lack of enthusiasm and involvement with her husband puts him in a vulnerable place. We have seen cases where the men very innocently find women who are willing to work by their side and are excited about their work. If these relationships are not dealt with, they could end in adultery. Another bit of advice is to have the wife approve of any female staff member who would be closely working with her husband. This will help her feel at ease when her husband has to spend long hours at the office.

Similarly, a woman with ministry involvements apart from her husband may find a more serious pattern developing. Often women are more interested in spiritual things than men. However, the man will often begrudge his wife's absence for ministry involvements. In this situation, this rule is to guide the wife: Scripturally, she must not be cut off from fellowship, but she does need to balance her ministry involvements considering the lack of involvement of her husband. (The same holds true in reverse.) Nevertheless, if the uninvolved husband professes to be a member of the Body, other leaders need to come to her aid and seek to build a fire under her husband!

Singles in Ministry

There is a great need for quality singles to fully give themselves to the Kingdom. We are aware of the problems of singles. Some are single not because of a true call to serve the Kingdom in this way, but because they are in a society where people fear growing up and making marriage commitments. This is endemic among the young men of our day. However, whether they are single by call or by default, singles are an extraordinary resource. First, singles are not tied to the same family hours as those who are married. Singles can excel in evangelism, follow up, service, fellowship, and other areas. They have time! However, singles need to stop thinking that life begins with marriage. In addition, singles need to keep attractive homes and practice hospitality. Yes, this includes single men.

I believe that some singles can perform well in significant leadership responsibilities. The unmarried Paul was an Apostle! I often wish I had someone without family responsibilities to send into a congregation in trouble for a few months. They could do so much in bringing healing and right government if they were trained and capable. Our short visits are sometimes comparatively inadequate. We can see why Paul extolled the potential of single life and singleness of devotion to the LORD and His Kingdom. Singles can also form service squads to aid widows, single parents, and the elderly in the many mundane tasks that are hard for them to do. Let us work to connect our singles to each other and to families and to enable them to go as far as their gifts and calling will allow. True, they may have difficulty relating to some struggles that married people and families have, but they can do so many other things better.

The Education of Leadership: Traditional Schools Verses Congregational Training

Many trained by the traditional seminary route are scandalized by the lack of Scriptural knowledge among those in leadership in the charismatic world. Errors such as out of context Scriptural interpretations and fantastic prophecies convince them that seminary is essential. On the other hand, those in leadership without this education are shocked by the skeptical attitude of the intellectually oriented seminary graduates. Their lack of moving in the Spirit, in faith, in power, and in practical impact seems to these folks to prove that seminary education is something to be avoided. I have been close friends with folks on both sides of this debate. There are really two problems in this debate, and many from both sides of the debate are beginning to see their one-sidedness.

First, traditional seminary education used to emphasize conveying intellectual knowledge without requiring the practical effectiveness of the student in ministry. Practical ministry quickly tests whether we have been equipped for ministry or only been filled with data like a computer. Without practical training during the years of seminary, too much knowledge will puff up. Many of our institutions were influenced by concepts of knowledge and skeptical attitudes from the enlightenment philosophies of the western world (from 18th century roots). These philosophies have pervaded our educational institutions for over 200 years. Often it is not exegetical accuracy that raises questions concerning charismatic experience, but the cultural presuppositions and the social context of the world of education. The problem is not education, but the humanistic enlightenment influence in education.

On the other hand, the prevalence of bad theology in the charismatic world proves that ignorance is not helpful to the Kingdom of God either. The LORD desires simplicity of faith, but not stupidity and gullibility. An accurate understanding of the Scriptures can be enhanced by the classroom, as can other patterns for learning for the ministry. Certainly our weakness as Americans is partially a function of the fact that people do not know the Scriptures. Instead of going to the Scripture for food, people assume the trustworthiness of a favored teacher to gain nourishment. This means that a basic education is not only needed by the minister but by the flock as well. Training in the Scriptures, whether by the congregation or seminary or other venues, is needed for all. Sound doctrine is one bulwark against error. Others are humility, fellowship, and a close devotional walk with the LORD.

I believe that every Scriptural training program needs to evaluate their presuppositions for training ministers. Is the theology of the school truly in accord with supernatural Scriptural perspectives, or has the school been subtly influenced by humanistic perspectives and the skepticism of enlightenment intellectualism? Are the faculty mere scholars, or righteous and effective members of the Body in witness and congregational life? Are the students genuinely involved in congregational life during seminary days and trained in practical responsibility while they study? Unless congregations and seminaries work together to achieve this ideal, the seminary will too often be the place for leaving the student spiritually dry and intellectually smug. Several years of intellectual orientation are not a balanced life. Only in real ministry does one maintain vital links to the Spirit that keep one solid in perspective. A heart for the LORD and His Kingdom is crucial. The model of being in a school apart from the battles of Kingdom life finds no support in the Scriptures.

However, those who emphasize practical training by coming up through the ranks need to realize the importance of education in the Scriptures. Handling the Scriptures accurately with the right principles of interpretation should be highly valued. The Union of Messianic Jewish Congregations endorses several schools that enable a high level of course work while remaining in ministry. This is the goal of the Messianic Jewish Bible Institutes, which have an accredited program with the King's University in California. Most of it can be done in online education. As noted, Messianic Jewish Bible Institute provides several short modules that can be very helpful in training leaders.

A More Ideal Model

I believe that a more ideal model can be developed by congregations in a region. They can band together to form a school that is an adjunct to the training of their members and leaders. It does not matter if the schooling part of the training takes longer. Many who graduate from formal educational structures hardly have a clue about how to pastor a growing congregation. Messiah Biblical University was our attempt to provide this model in a suburb north of Washington, D.C. Messianic Jewish leaders, scholars, and pastors from the local area taught in our school. The students were sent to us by their congregations (churches in the local area and Messianic Jewish congregations and churches from other areas) to provide an adjunct to their training in congregational life. In addition, Messianic Jewish leaders came from various parts of the country to join our congregations and our school for the practical and intellectual training needed.

I believe that we will see seminaries transformed to become regional church training centers as the LORD restores His Body to unity. Furthermore, I believe we will see more schools like Messiah Biblical University and Buffalo Bible Institute (a similar regional school). If we could transcend our denominational differences and join in restored Church models, training both intellectually and practically could be localized. For those called to be scholars, elite centers could be maintained or created. However, most Scriptural training institutions could become local and trans-denominational. They would support the restoration models of congregational life described in this manual.

What about the Para-Church?

The Scriptures do not present us significant models for para-congregational ministry. The New Testament seems to assume that most of the work needed in spreading the Gospel and discipling will take place on the congregational level and by traveling teams under apostolic leaders. Traveling teams in the first century are the closest thing in the Scriptures to para-church ministries.

A few years ago, a well-known para-congregational leader told me that he had come to the conclusion that effective, ongoing evangelism would not be effectively done at the congregational level. The congregational structure was necessary for community and discipleship in his view, but effective evangelism required the para-congregational organization. Those who have worked on both sides of the congregational and para-congregational divide have noted mistrust, lack of cooperation, and even competition sometimes cropping up. Having observed these organizations for over thirty years, I do have some thoughts.

Much that the para-congregational organization does could be done congregationally if congregations were truly ministry equipping centers as Ephesians 4:11 notes. There are models of congregational life that are more effective than any para-congregation could ever be in many areas. I believe that the existence of some para-congregational organizations is due to the mercy of the LORD in providing an alternative because congregations are not fulfilling their Scripturally enjoined roles.

Functions beyond a Local Congregation are Needed

There are functions needed for equipping and spreading the Gospel that are too much for any local congregational unit. Congregations connect in associations, which form sending boards, oversee radio broadcasts, and sponsor traveling bands. Sometimes associations of congregations are lacking in vision, so the work is done outside their structure. However, I do believe it would be more ideal if much that the para-church does was carried on by boards of oversight that were accountable to congregations and congregational associations. Some functions may even be overseen by representatives of several associations and thus tied to Scriptural congregational roots. Why is this important? It is because Yeshua gave authority to His "kehilah" congregation (congregational leaders) not to His para-congregation. However, I consider traveling teams, planting teams, and inter-congregational ministries to be expressions of congregations! I would not call them para-congregational. It is well for the eldership boards of inter-congregational ministries to include elder representatives who have expertise in varieties of needed gifts

49

and talents (lawyers, pastors and businessmen). If these folks are truly committed to congregational life, they will structure the ministry so that it is rightly rooted, and not competing with or undercutting local congregations.

Even with these considerations, there are necessary organizations that legally cannot be under congregations. These would include legal aid associations, commercial broadcast associations, political associations, and lobbying groups. These would be overseen by boards of mature members of the Body who are experts in the particular areas of concern. In addition, there are specialized communities that define membership to very specific definitions of purpose. These are called *sodalities* by church missiologists. Training bases, for instance with Youth with a Mission or Gatways Beyond, are communities that fit this definition. This can be quite legitimate as long as there are real elders and the people recognize eldership authority while part of this training *sodality*.

We do not live in an ideal world and probably will continue to have congregations and para-congregations – neither of which fit the ideal. How do we foster cooperation and maximize the potential for extending the Kingdom of God? I believe that the primary issue between the congregation and the para-congregation is the issue of authority. To whom is a person primarily accountable for spiritual correction and discipline? Who has the primary right to rebuke, correct and disfellowship from the Body? The answer to this question defines membership. If a para-congregation considers itself to have this authority, it should be overseen by a plurality of real, Scriptural elders. It then is a special kind of congregation. Indeed, the members of the apostolic traveling bands in the New Testament seem to be primarily accountable to the leaders of the bands. However, many para-congregations are not organized to provide discipleship, elder oversight, or discipline on this level. If not, its staff must be solidly part of the life of a congregation just as a person in any other vocation.

Defining Commitments and Jurisdiction

Often the problem of tension arises because a para-congregational organization and a congregation do not define their relationship to the people who are part of the paid staff or volunteer staff of the para-congregation who also attend congregational functions. This leaves such a person into a no man's land – with both organizations making claims upon his time and loyalty. There are only two valid options. One is that the para-congregational group sees that it is a specific expression of the Body under an eldership. Its staff and designated volunteers have their primary membership in this group. Discipline will be primarily under the leadership of this organization. In this case the staff member can attend a congregation, if the supplement is needed. The congregation can accept the person's primary involvement and accountability as being in the other organization. His or her attendance will be like an associate member. The second option is that primary discipline and accountability is to the congregation, but that the person has a vocation expressed in the para-congregational organization. In the latter case, the para-congregational organization will release the staff member to be sufficiently involved in the life of the congregation. Furthermore, it will be made clear to the elders of the congregation that they have full membership oversight of this staff member. Both can work together as situations arise. However, every person is called to define accountability to a real eldership that is keeping watch over the souls of the members.

CHAPTER 4

Administrative Order and Balance

Everyone to some extent is called to administration. This does not mean that everyone has the gift of administration. However, every individual must govern their time and complete their responsibilities. Fathers must administrate the family. They delegate tasks and follow up with their spouse and their children. Mothers are called to administration in the home as well. This requires time management, delegating chores, and financial management in shopping. The husband and wife should normally agree upon who will be responsible for which areas of oversight in the home. The husband is the executive director or president of the family and the mother the vice-president. Therefore, we teach that all need to learn management at a basic level.

Members of our congregations usually find themselves in situations where conflicting claims seem to be made upon their time and money. For example, parents have to deal with quality time given to children, to their spouse, to friends, to parents, and their relatives. What time should they give to congregational service, to political and social responsibility, to the work world or economic sphere, or to recreation? And then there is the concern to serve the lost which is a key to evangelism. Even this incomplete list may make some people anxious. However, this is a trustworthy statement: "From the LORD's point of view, there are no conflicts of priority in our lives." From the LORD's point of view, conflicts of priorities are always the result of not discerning the will of the LORD for the use of our time and money. Like Yeshua, we are to only give ourselves to what the Father is doing (John 5:19). Therefore, we can say that the most important element in good administration from a Scriptural point of view is a continuous and close fellowship with the LORD. Yeshua is our example; He was never confused about His priorities. We cannot attain to the perfection of Yeshua, but we can make progress toward His example.

The Demands of People

Another factor in good administration that follows the leading of the Spirit is to not be subject to the demands of people. This is most clearly seen in the request from the family of Lazarus (John 11). The delay of Yeshua seemed unreasonable. Yet His delay was necessary for the glory of the LORD to be seen in the greatest gospel miracle outside His own resurrection. Do we minister to the crowds or spend time with the woman at the well? Do we spend time in quiet prayer or do we share with the disciples? Can we see that the extraordinary anointing upon Yeshua drew great crowds? It also tempted people to make great demands upon Him. I do not believe that the His challenge related to time management was less than our challenge. One of the greatest sources of burn out is seeking to meet the demands and expectations of people. This is often motivated by the fear of man. The minister wants to be loved and accepted by the people. He also really loves them and wants to meet their needs. If the demands of the people become our rule for involvement, we will surely be displeasing to the LORD. We are to walk in love at all times. However, the dispensing of that love to various people at various times is by the leading of the Spirit. That we have a heart of love toward someone may not mean that we spend large amounts of time with that person.

Having stated the general principle, however, we have to balance what we say with the fact that a successful minister generally follows a pattern of time management and administrative order. Yes, this can at any time be suspended by the leading of the Spirit. On the other hand, we have to be very wary of the "charismatic" style of subjectivity that leads to irresponsibility. If the normal pattern of administrative responsibility is being constantly suspended with the claim that the Spirit is leading, something is wrong. These words are valid for all members and leaders at every level of responsibility.

It is important to teach the membership on the importance of responsible Scriptural living. This teaching must be included as a central part of the claim of Yeshua upon us by His sacrifice. The power of grace in the Holy Spirit to energize and enable, and the importance of living according to the pattern of life seen in the Scriptures, should be emphasized if we want our people to walk in the joy and blessing of the LORD.

Time Management and the Use of a Calendar

Calendars and related tools give us a sense of the rhythm of our lives and enable us to see whether we have included too many commitments or, as is rarely the case, too little. Note that often the primary problem with ministers is that they are busy with the wrong things.

The most significant tool in time management is a good calendar system. A good system will have planning calendars for both monthly and annual scheduling. It will also have space for daily appointments. We have found that the best calendar system for the money in paper form is available from Day-Timers, in Altoona, Pennsylvania. The Day-Timers system costs about $35 per year and includes the materials sold in other systems that cost over $150.

It includes different formats for different needs. There are note taking sheets, delegation and follow up sheets, task "to do" sheets, tax record sheets for business deductions, and many more. It also includes planning calendars so that a year at a glance, a month at a glance, and a week at a glance can be easily contemplated. Today this calendar system is available in electronic form. Most today do prefer this. In addition, many standard programs from either Apple or Microsoft include calendar planning. They are generally very good and include lists and planning tools as well. I recommend sampling different systems before choosing.

Annual Calendars

Step number one in calendar planning is to deal with the year at a glance. Where is vacation time to be placed? What annual events or conferences will we attend? What are the special anniversaries or birthdays to be included? Where are the holidays that will require my family time or congregational participation? These dates should be filled in on the annual calendar. The annual calendar also includes special leadership retreats and any events that occur quarterly or less frequently. As important as these dates are, planning times for the annual events for which a leader has responsibility are as crucial. Let us remember, however, our goal is that all members will responsibly manage their time. The difference between non-leadership members and various levels of leadership is that higher leadership entails broader servant-hood responsibility. For example, the leader will not only block out the Day of Atonement or Passover-Resurrection season, but he will block out the planning time for these events some months in advance. He will also make sure that those who are to plan with him have these dates on their calendar.

Monthly Calendar

The dates chosen for the annual calendar should be then transferred to a monthly calendar in the calendar system. Thus when we plan the normal month, we will not inadvertently produce conflicts of scheduling. Monthly calendar planning includes such things as the monthly leadership meetings, monthly elders meetings, the monthly pastors' fellowship in the local area, and other events that occur once a week or less. The monthly calendar is the place to block out special days off with the family and friends. Some annual events are shared with family and friends as well.

Weekly Calendar

The monthly calendar is then transferred to the weekly calendar that has every day divided into hourly slots. For most people, the system that allows the whole week to be seen at a glance is the best. A page per day causes too many to not see the larger period of a week for better weekly planning. Electronic calendar systems make this very easy as one simply moves from the monthly calendar, to a weekly screen, and then a day screen – a simple point-and-click does this. The same can be accomplished by going from the Day-Timer monthly paper calendar to week and day sheets.

The weekly calendar will include the information from the annual planning calendar, the monthly calendar, and things only planned in the immediate for that week. This calendar reflects a weekly rhythm of life for a normal week and a different rhythm for weeks when monthly and annual dates are part of a specific week. There are two normal patterns of life for people. One is the pattern for people who are in full time ministry, and the other for people who are in the business or other vocational worlds. I will outline these patterns.

First, I want to say that planning is to be done prayerfully and with a flexible orientation. Opportunities will come up which require us to change the originally written plans. When they do, we need to ask a question. If the new opportunity is to be accepted, what will be done with the responsibilities originally planned? Either we can decide that they are not important and cancel them, or we can reschedule. However, rescheduling should be immediately done and reflected on all the calendars where applicable: annual, monthly, and weekly. Why? It is far too easy to be irresponsible and to say, "Oh well, I will fit it in somewhere later when the time comes." This is a prescription for disaster. For example, if the conflict is with planning for the High Holidays, a Messianic Jewish leader better reschedule this in plenty of time. To be irresponsible here is indeed not wise!

If it requires rescheduling a leadership gathering, the leader needs to be sure that the opportunity is very significant, undertaken by the leading of the LORD, and that most people can reschedule to be with him at the new leadership gathering time.

More about the Daily Schedule

I always keep a small pad in my pocket to write down thoughts I want to tell others, tasks I have to do, ideas, or dates to be remembered. On a regular basis, I then go through my pad and transfer the items I wrote down to the appropriate page in my Day-Timer: the "to do" page, or daily-monthly schedule. I still really like the simple memo pads and have been using them for over 50 years. However, today there are electronic pads and "to do" lists on most smart phones. Most young people prefer this.

It is a good idea to pray over the "to do" list every morning and decide which tasks the LORD wants you to accomplish for that day or what tasks are to be delegated. When you know that you have heard from the LORD, you can believe that there will be enough time to complete all the tasks on your list and not get into anxiety. If the LORD has spoken, the job will be accomplished! No matter what their calling, this method can be used by both men and women, whether in ministry or not. When I had less responsibility, I considered myself caught up when there were 15 items on my "to do" list. With today's responsibilities on my "to do" list, I consider myself caught up at 25 items. Also, I keep a medium term list and a long term list. I periodically read over these lists and transfer some of them to the "to do" list. This way I do some things that I really want to eventually accomplish, even though they are not urgent.

A Normal Week for Members

What does a normal week look like for a member or leader not in full time ministerial vocations? First, the person needs to block out family times. There should be an evening and an afternoon or day given over to family every week. Sometimes these times can include intimate friends, but quality with the family is the emphasis. In our family, this was usually Saturday or Sunday afternoon and another evening. In Israel this tends to be part of Friday and part of Saturday. Furthermore, dinner times are crucial for family coherence. We require all members of our family to eat together most evenings unless there are prearranged excuses. We are glad for family time. Our children in our first edition of this book spanned the ages of eight to nineteen years old. In our family, we usually took two hours (6pm-8pm) from before dinner to evening for family time. There are exceptions, but even then we tried to have dinner together and tried to get from 1-1.5 hours of quality time. We were consistent in this for over 17 years. It was an anchor of relationship in the flux of changing schedules. Today our children are following such patterns with their children, who at the time of this writing consist of 8 grandchildren ranging from 1-13 years old.

The person we are describing will normally be up early in the morning for devotions. Any mature believe will spend at least an hour most days before the LORD. Then men and women who work will have breakfast and be off to work. Mothers who are able will be at home to do the tasks of running a home and raising a family, to have time for prayer and the Scriptures, to reach out to others, etc. Mothers with vocational commitments outside the home will be putting in their normal eight to nine hours a day at work. They will be using child care. Finding time for devotions, home responsibilities, and family care becomes much more challenging. If husbands and wives shared the work and each worked 30 hours a week, there could be a good pattern. I think we have to question the idea of families with pre-high school children having both parents working and together putting in from 80-100 hours per week.

Here is a challenge for our day. It is the spirit of our age to swallow up people in the economic sector. High tech workers are sometimes made to work 70-80 hours a week. The Kingdom will progress little through people who put in inordinate hours in the work world. We teach that all need to come to the place of faith where the economic sphere is brought into line. This is the Sabbath principle. We encourage all to study the Scriptures on the meaning of the Sabbath and to see that time is to be spent responsibly, just as we seek the LORD on how to spend our money. As people begin a faith walk with the LORD regarding their money in tithing, so they respectfully put their foot down with employers and set standards for their time. At a certain point, faith will have to be built for this stand to be taken. (We believe that it is very important to teach the flock to tithe and deal with their money by faith as in *Growing to Maturity*, our discipleship guide.) Our attitude to the work sphere is, "If I perish, I perish; but the LORD will provide and see that I can provide for my family within reasonable time commitments." This is the Sabbath principle. We can take a stand in faith and expect the LORD to come through for us if our motive is the Kingdom. We do not have to be slaves to the economic sphere.

Congregation and Witness

Key involvements in congregational activities for most people take place after work and on weekends. How should time be spent? Some evenings will be given to ministry. This will include serving lost people, discipling others, being discipled, and serving others in the community. Not every evening will be the same. Weekend time can be given for these involvements as well. Also included should be time for study of the Scriptures. The limits of time may preclude all these things being part of a weekly pattern, but they can be part of an every other week or monthly pattern. Slots should also be blocked out for special times of prayer, both individually and as families. It was an axiom of Beth Messiah Congregation that the work of the Congregation is largely carried out between 7:30-10pm weeknights along with weekend hours.

What about recreation? Yes, recreation led by the LORD can be scheduled too. Recreation times can be fellowship times for family and friends. However, frivolous recreation of much television is simply not an option for Kingdom life. A special and valuable program – yes. But a Kingdom life simply will not leave room for worthless, passive entertainment.

We also seek to teach our members that the Kingdom is extended by the quality of their lives on the job (in their vocation) including the quality of their service to fellow workers or peers. Kingdom advancement is made through their personal witness of speaking the good news of the gospel as the LORD leads. There is time for the responsibilities outlined here. Many of our members live this Kingdom life!

It should be noted that some callings or vocations will not allow for this normal pattern. The politician, the doctor with evening hours, and the counselor may not be able to work the normal workday hours. If the calling to these professions is genuine, the congregation needs to establish support groups that fit the schedule of such professionals (lunch times, early mornings, etc.). These folks need quality support, exhortation, and accountability too.

It is important that our congregation not become isolated from the world around us. Integration into the larger society and serving those who do not know Yeshua is important. People can also participate in Jewish Community Centers, clubs, reading circles, and other venues where we develop relationships with those who do not know Yeshua. Only so will we expand the Kingdom.

A Pattern for a Full Time Ministerial Vocation

What is the pattern of life for a full time vocation minister? Amazingly, the pattern for members and full-time ministers from dinner to bedtime is about the same. The primary difference is in the day time hours. Normally, we encourage ministers to give their mornings to devotional life, prayer, Scriptural study, and teaching preparation. Some afternoon time can be spent as well on preparation. However, there are also times for early morning pastor's prayer gatherings in the locality, staff gatherings, and even pastoral or staff retreats on weekdays. These last are part of annual calendar planning. However, the full-time minister is free to pursue a host of afternoon involvements at the leading of the LORD. There is the administration of the congregation that entails office hours. There is the potential for lunch appointments of an evangelistic nature or of a shepherding nature. There are hospital visits, and there may be volunteer work to serve lost people. The gym or community center is another place to meet people and maintain an exercise program. Some follow up or delegation can be done in the afternoon, including working with staff and calling leaders at work who have employment (if a quick phone call is not a problem for them). This is a time to follow up with the women coordinators of various ministry areas who are not working in the business world.

Evening time after the family hour will usually be given to ministry. The nature of involvements will vary with gifts and responsibilities. The head minister will give his evenings primarily to meet with leaders and spouses who are shepherding or coordinating major areas of congregational life such as evangelism or follow up. Sometimes two or three couples can meet together on the same evening. They can share on the challenges of congregational life, the health of their marriages and families, and other topics that will aid them in fulfilling their callings. Once a few home cell groups are successfully operating, the senior leader will have little time to meet with members. He will primarily spend time with leaders who can be trained to counsel and equip members. He will visit cell groups. Eventually, when a board of elder peers is in place, he will oversee them in their task of overseeing several home cell groups.

Evenings will also be spent in evangelism. Perhaps the senior leader will join a book discussion group or other community activities. I believe that it is important that the senior leader set an example in having some time in his life given to serving and winning lost people. It is not impossible. This has been part of my life despite significant local and trans-local activities. With the leadership training evenings, day retreats and special prayer meetings, the senior leader's time will be full.

Patterns for Elders and Cell Leaders

Elders and cell group leaders will have similar schedules, but they will be meeting with different groups of people. The elders will meet with the intern couple of the cell they oversee and with the leaders of the other cells they oversee. Home cell leaders will meet with their cell group's interns and will meet with other cell members in informal groups for fellowship and social bonding. He will meet with others in the cell that are farther along in discipling others and reaching lost people but have not yet progressed to the intern stage.

As the reader can see, there is a pattern of regularly meeting with people who are above us in authority and with people below us on the leadership flow chart! Thus, bonds are formed between members and leaders in their cells. The leaders of cells are linked to overseers of two to five cells. Overseers of two to five cells (elders) are linked with each other and with the leader over 25 cells. Linking, bonding, and accountability are part of the structure all the way up and all the way down. Significant coordinators, of ministries beyond cell life, meet with deacon and elder overseers. It is important to have periodic sharing times for peers with spouses present. This mutual support is important in keeping our lives whole and sharp for the LORD. At Beth Messiah we obtained 12 solid cells and had 90% of our members attending cells regularly. However, this pattern works with a small congregation of just one module of five cell, as well as huge congregations with hundreds of cells, such as in Boris Greshenko's congregation in Kiev, Ukraine. This is the largest Messianic Jewish congregation in the world with 1,600 people as of this writing. This model has also worked for various other international congregations.

This cannot happen unless there is a balance assured by solid calendar planning. Cell members and leaders are also to be giving themselves to serving lost people. Family, serving the people in the congregation, serving the lost, and the "household tasks" of the community are all to be undertaken responsibly in the balance of the leading of the Holy Spirit. It is all based upon the quality of our devotional life including individual and corporate worship.

We cannot urge the reader too much; it is crucial that you understand that ministry success will be greatly dependent on two things. The first and foremost is the quality of your walk with the LORD resulting in healthy relationships. The second is a disciplined life of time management.

Delegation Follow up and Administrative Flow

A task can often metaphorically fit the saying, "Out of sight, out of mind." Tasks are often assigned to another and then forgotten. This will ensure that many important things will not be done. Furthermore, a capable leader knows that the time management standards set above cannot be fulfilled unless there is rigorous commitment to two things. First, the leader cannot be available to all who want his involvement, when they want it. This will mean managing the phone. Second, the capable leader needs to know what he is called to do and what he is called to delegate. Delegation will often be determined by the official roles of coordination. A task for the Sabbath school will be given to the Sabbath school coordinator.

Let's first deal with the issue of availability. In the early stage of a congregation, perhaps 20-30 people, the head leader can be generally available to the whole flock. Even then, this does not mean being available at every hour. Total availability means unavailability to the tasks and involvements that are really given to us by the LORD, including time with the LORD Himself. It is foolish to think that people only request our time at the LORD's promptings. The totally available leader of even a small congregation will find his family life suffering. His spiritual life will suffer as well. I have not always practiced what I have written. I well remember the great disappointment that would come over the faces of my children when the phone would ring during the dinner hour or the family time hour. The congregation came first. I was in bondage to the fear of man, my desire to lovingly meet needs, and the old school teaching that said that if I really loved my flock, I would be available to any member any time night or day. The factor of the telephone made this availability standard a true tyranny, since picking up and dialing was much easier than hiking to the leader's home.

At the early stage of planting, there is often no secretary-receptionist and no office outside the home. In my early years of ministry, my wife was my secretary. Together we were the pastors, newsletter editors, the mail team (before computers we ran the old addressograph and the mimeograph!), the education directors, the fellowship leaders, and more. Even so, a planter is a jack of all trades. At this point, the key management decision is to have a phone answering machine. However, total unavailability is not good either. I believe that leaders should keep general hours in which they do answer the phone. What I am putting forth here is a practical orientation for home cell leaders as well. When the return calls become too much, it is good for the voicemail system to encourage people to call back during office hours. During office hours, if one is counseling and does not want to be interrupted, the voicemail system can encourage people to leave a message. A voicemail system with a variety of message types for different circumstances (for vacation, holidays, requesting a call back later, requesting to leave a message) is an extraordinary tool.

As a congregation grows, the general availability of the head leader to the whole flock must necessarily decrease. Of course, exceptions are made in tragedies and real emergencies. In the larger congregation, the leader's time is given to the leadership team. This change of priorities begins early in the planting stage. As cell leaders are raised up, calls will come first to the cell leaders and not the senior pastor. It is well to train a flock of thirty with two cells to this habit. The head leader is still available, but this is the weaning period. In our counsel, we encourage the leader to take no morning calls, to practice afternoon office hours, and to have some evening hours. These hours can be publicized. I have found an opposite pattern to be very frustrating to fellow members and other leaders, whereby the leader seems to never be available with no dependable pattern of office hours. He is unlikely to be reached by anyone! This is a pattern that progressively concerns me. I have seen this extreme too often as well.

When the calls become too many due to a growing flock, other steps can be taken to limit phone tyranny. Having two phones can be a real help. One is a public phone and the other private. The private phone number is given to leaders and close friends. It is used for emergencies or friendship. Members can call others from the leadership team that can contact the head pastor. The publicly listed phone will be answered when desirable or hooked up to the machine. The flock will experience the level of unavailability that the leader puts forth and will tailor their response accordingly. Because the head leader is only available in a larger congregation to a limited degree, they will call other leaders. However, if time permits, I am willing to take calls from anyone who calls during office hours.

It is hard to imagine how much difference is made to a congregation when there is a secretary-receptionist. A part time person can be hired during afternoon office hours for 20 hours a week. This person can screen calls, route calls to the proper coordinator, do correspondence and the basic newsletter-bulletin. Records and filing are crucial skills. A disorganized secretary is a disaster. Be careful here.

Flow Charts

As a congregation develops, it will revise its flow charts. Such a chart is important. It reminds the leader of who is responsible for what areas so that he does not unthinkingly take on tasks and undercut the one to whom coordination has been delegated. It is also important for the congregation. This information gives them the sense of the organizational structure and whom to call for various concerns. In the early stage of congregational life, the head leader is at the top of the chart and the coordinators report to him on their responsibilities regularly. Monthly meetings and follow up calls are attainable. However, in a larger congregation, the elders will coordinate various areas of congregational life and also oversee the deacons who coordinate areas of ministry as well. One can see by this that elders are those who can bear a significant weight of governmental responsibility. A congregation of a larger size, let's say 150-400 can be managed by the elders with the pastor. Staff numbers vary according to building style. A congregation can usually support one pastoral person per 100 members, but this is not a fixed proportion since the tasks in a congregation of 400 are not always twice that of a congregation of 200.

The deacons will give reports of their areas of responsibility to the elder who oversees them. The elders will make reports of all areas of congregational life at the elders meeting. It is also possible to invite deacon coordinators to the elders meeting to make reports directly. This saves time, in contrast to requiring the pastor to moderate another meeting for the deacon board.

Record Keeping

Most successful congregations require their cell leaders to keep records. These records are turned into the overseers who are over groups of cells. These statistics are essential in enabling the leadership to know what is happening in the community. It is helpful for leaders to keep records on those who have come to the LORD and information on where members are serving. Also, keeping track of what courses members are taking, or training they are receiving, is important for adequately equipping people for doing the works of ministry. Surveys of the needs of members are also helpful. Sometimes the LORD can use this to show where preaching and teaching is needed. W. Steven Brown's book *13 Fatal Errors Managers Make and How You Can Avoid Them* is the best small book I have read on administrative principles. We note his basic chapter headings here just to give you some idea of his book, noting the fatal errors:

1) Refuse to Accept Personal Accountability
2) Fail to Develop People
3) Try to Control Results Instead of Influencing Thinking

4) Join the Wrong Crowd
5) Manage Everyone the Same Way
6) Forget the Importance of Profit
7) Concentrate on Problems Rather Than Objectives
8) Be a Buddy, not a Boss
9) Fail to Set Standards
10) Fail to Train Your People
11) Condone Incompetence
12) Recognize Only Top Performers
13) Try to Manipulate People

Similar principles are put forth in more recent books like Jim Collin's *Good to Great*, which is applied to congregations in Thom S. Rainer's *Breakout Churches*. I mention these here for training home group leaders, but later I will mention key business books that are a great help for building congregations. The principles are universal.

One of the sad errors in some parts of the charismatic world is to despise organization. This is a tragic error. If we do not organize, we will accomplish little. In this regard, the apostles saw the need to appoint deacons. The purpose is to have organizations that are relationship based, organic, and formed by the Spirit's leading. We must use our organization and not let our organization use us. Furthermore, we must be willing to change as needs arise and to not deify our organization. Poor organization is simply irresponsibility masquerading as spirituality. Organization must never replace the power of the Spirit, but the Spirit will lead us to embrace responsible organization.

Long Range Planning

It is important to set forth goals for the congregation, with the counsel and agreement of the elders. These goals are birthed in prayer. We also strongly recommend seeking the confirmation of the congregation for these goals so that all are in unity together. What is the vision for the congregation for the coming year? What are the goals that we believe by faith we can accomplish? What are the goals for the next five years? How will we get there? These goals will only be partially met. However if there is not significant attainment, then we are not really walking in faith and responsibility. The late John Wimber's Vineyard International publishes an excellent planning workbook for aiding in this task. It is called the "5 Year Planner." Here are some examples of goals for beginning congregations and for larger congregations. We will pick a Messianic Jewish congregation and its outreach orientation. However, any other orientation can easily apply this. Here are some first year goals:

1) Join Jewish discussion groups to befriend and serve Jewish people
2) Advertise first cell group meetings using newspapers, Christian radio public service announcements, posters, and flyers
3) Inform all Evangelical Congregations in a 10 mile radius of availability to help with Jewish ministry and desire to cooperate and be helpful
4) See first cell grow to twenty people and divide into two cells
5) See cells multiply to three cells and begin traveling to each cell
6) Begin regular Sabbath services and meet regularly for the second half of the year
7) Train all cell members in basic Scriptural doctrine (of Kingdom life) and in serving lost people
8) Ordain first deacons at the end of the year (presumably the end of year 2-3 for first possible elders)

Here are some goals for the next year:

1) See cells multiply from 3 to 6 cells
2) See that all cell leaders are responsible in reporting and communication

3) See half of the members involved in some ministry of serving lost people
4) See a large proportion of members involved in Jewish community activities
5) Attain $200,000 in building fund toward breaking ground
6) Revise Sabbath school teacher training and significantly raise level of teacher ability

A planning orientation for five years puts forth the goals to be accomplished within five years and then breaks down the level of attainment planned by the end of year two, three, and four. These goal and planning exercises are important in keeping one focused.

Delegation and Follow Up

Delegating and following up is a crucial skill. First is the general delegation from the senior leader or the board of elders to the various coordinators. Each coordinator should be given a job description. They should be encouraged to pray for vision in their area of oversight. Vision and direction should then be approved by the elders. With elder approval they may change the job description as they find more useful ways to proceed. It is crucial that regular communication takes place in regular reports through the elder overseer – to the senior leader if necessary, and to the board of overseers.

However, beyond such general delegation, there is specific delegation. Cell group leaders delegate to their interns and to other members of the cell group. The overseer of five cells does the same. The Superintendent of the Sabbath School delegates to the teachers in the Sabbath School. The senior leader delegates to associate staff leaders and to the administrators or secretaries. The whole structure we speak of here requires that we motivate people to be responsible and that we train them in how to be responsible.

We live in a day of unusual irresponsibility. Therefore, it will often be the case that a leader will find it easier to do it himself. This will be true over the short haul. However, it will be more difficult over the long haul. Furthermore, such a decision of "doing it myself" will hinder the raising up of responsible members and leaders. Our job is not to take the easy short cut but to use the system of delegation and service to train people to be responsible. Prayer and motivation by Scriptural precepts are very important in the motivational task. For unpaid workers there is no fear of losing a job or a deduction in pay. So this motive for paid staff challenges us to find other motivations.

A day in the life of a busy pastor requires many assignments to be delegated. Here are a few examples. Delegate to the associate pastor the responsibility to follow up on a false prophecy received in the mail and to get back to the senior leader on it. Delegate to the secretary to call the elders and remind them of the special elders retreat day. Delegate to the education superintendent the job to remind all teachers to be teaching on the fall feasts during August. Delegate to the secretary to call the leader of the pastor's fellowship for an RSVP to a dinner planned in October. Delegate to the retreat administrator to locate the retreat facility for the summer, prepare a list of costs, and prepare a breakdown of suggested registration fees. Delegated assignments need to be clear on deadlines and priorities. Often, responsible servants are not good judges of what the priorities are if several assignments are given.

There are two excellent tools for delegation. For office staff, memos with copy paper are very helpful. Each task can be outlined with the deadline. The original is given to the person who is to carry out the task. The copy is kept by the delegating leader. Regularly the leader should go through all the copies and follow up. Follow up is the name of the game. It is wise to set deadlines ahead of the actual date if necessary. If the task is not completed, follow up can make sure that it will be done.

Who are the people who are being raised to be coordinators and governing leaders? One test for candidates for leadership is that they carry out their delegated tasks responsibly and with little follow up. In addition, a good training method for potential leaders is to give them tasks that require them to work with persons under them and to delegate to them.

The other tool for delegation is the "delegation follow-up" list. Day-Timers publish an excellent grid sheet for their calendar system. Electronic calendar-management systems also have delegation and follow up grid sheets. Space is included for the date the task is given, to whom the task is given, the description of the task, the date due, and a check off for when the task is completed.

The tools of motivation used in the business world are valid, but they should be used under the leading and direction of the Spirit. Praise and gratitude for those who carry out tasks responsibly is important. Public recognition can be appropriate for those who are truly responsible servants and servant leader coordinators. However, praise should be genuine and not manipulative. The leader should be truly thankful for those who help in the attainment of Kingdom goals.

It is also important to correct and lovingly rebuke those who are irresponsible. When a people accept a task and do not carry it out responsibly, or when people coordinating an area handle it poorly, they must be corrected. We serve the King of Kings. Perhaps the coordinators need more training in their roles. If this is the problem, the leader needs to be quite understanding and loving. However, if the problem is irresponsibility, the consequences need to be explained with loving exhortation to do better. Irresponsibility can be egregious. Procrastination and simply dropping the ball need stronger correction. Having genuine excuses, but not informing the leader-delegator, is less serious. However, the failure to communicate is a serious problem. Lastly, people may be unable to fulfill the task because of other circumstances that make it the LORD's will that they not complete the task. If possible, they should aid the leader in finding another responsible leader to fulfill the task.

Monkeys and Organizational Delegation

One leader of sixteen congregations in Maryland gave a seminar on monkeys and administration. I was privileged to attend this presentation several years ago. "Monkeys" were defined as tasks to be done or delegated. A leader has a choice for every task. Does he delegate it or attempt to do it himself? He needs to weigh whether this task really should be done. What will maximize the ultimate extension of the Kingdom to the greatest extent? A leader who gives a task away is said to "give away a monkey." To take care of the task is called "feeding the monkey." The concept of monkeys is a helpful memory tool. First, monkeys do need to be taken care of. They need to be fed or they will become hungry. If they are not fed, they will starve and can potentially die. Then they will stink. When a person receives a monkey, he either needs to take care of it or give it to someone else to take care of. If he cannot find someone to take care of it, perhaps he should return the monkey to the one who gave it to him. However, monkeys seek to climb to the top (the head leader), and we need to try to see that monkeys are taken care of without doing this. Sometimes it will be seen that it is not necessary to have a particular monkey at all. It must be shot and given a decent burial.

This allegory is really quite clear. Indeed a task needs to be clearly assigned and taken care of by the person who receives it. If it is not taken care of it will cause problems. Like a hungry monkey, it will make noise and cause disturbances. If it is not eventually taken care of it can really create a big problem (a stinking monkey). Sometimes, a person does have to return the delegated task to the delegator. However, early communication is crucial rather than just ignoring the task completely. There needs to be time to re-delegate and not just drop the task. Only the delegator who originated the task can decide if the particular task can afford to be eliminated. It is important to have tasks delegated so that head leaders are free to do what they do best for the community. Those in the down-line of delegation will often try to delegate up to the leadership, but leaders need to be rigorous in always pushing tasks down the ranks into the community.

This allegory can be presented to the larger leadership and even the congregation in a lovely skit with stuffed monkeys held by members of the cast. All of the variations can be acted out.

A moderate size congregation delegates its tasks through the structures established. To not do so is to undercut the coordinators established. When people come to leaders and avoid the coordinators who are set up to handle areas of congregational life, they are ignoring the leaders' requests to flow within the congregational structure. When a leader carries out plans without consulting the person established as a coordinator in the area, he also undercuts the authority and excitement of the person in that area.

A normal flow chart for a moderate size congregation is shown below. Please note that a congregation develops toward this in stages.

Senior Pastor
Elders

John Smith – Elder	Paul Jones – Elder	Bill Cohen – Elder	Al Stein - Elder
Education Supervisor	Youth Director	Evangelism Director	Social Action
Worship Leader	College-Careers	Helps Ministry	Treasurer
Singles Ministry	Welfare Ministry	Women's ministry	Fellowship

Here we see each elder oversees three coordinators who report to him regularly – and through him to the board. The senior pastor is in touch with the necessary areas of congregational life through the elder board and through communication with individual elders. Regular communication and encouragement to others to be responsible throughout the structure are crucial.

Beyond the oversight of these coordinators, the elders will oversee five cell groups. The senior leader and elders may delegate to the coordinators. Some tasks are best handled in cell groups. The senior leader may also delegate to the coordinators through the elders. Coordinators in turn delegate to those who work under them. Some senior leaders burn themselves out because they have a structure of all coordinators reporting directly to them. This is not at all necessary. However, one can see by this that the elders need to bear a significant weight of responsibility for the community. When there are *shamashim* (deacons), they can oversee areas of responsibility and report to elders.

Financial Management and Disclosure

It is crucial to see that the treasurer and pastor of a congregation work with a trained accountant to set up a system of solid financial management and bookkeeping. The categories should be according to the normal spending patterns of congregations. One of the important issues is that the miscellaneous category should be a very small figure for expenses that simply were not anticipated under other categories. Salaries, benefits, rents, office expenses, missions giving, benevolence, and educational expenses are clearly demarcated.

The elders set the spending priorities. The treasurer sees that the elders maintain the spending according to the levels set in each category. Congregational spending should reflect its vision. Budgeting and planning meetings of the elders need to ask the question of how the spending is in accord with the vision of the community. The treasurer works with an accountant to see that all legal and taxation issues are properly handled.

Solid financial management with integrity of spending and record keeping is essential. This includes having some sense of proper proportions in spending, proper staff salaries, and disclosure to the congregation. It is crucial to keep everything legal and clear regarding government regulations as well. You must be prepared in case you are ever investigated, as has been happening more and more in a world that is turning against the LORD.

It is important that financial management be ultimately under a board of leaders who have integrity and are willing to provide real accountability. In the planting stage when such elders are not present, this function can be fulfilled by extra-congregational pastors and elders. There should never be a stage where there is no plurality of accountability. The board of accountability should receive monthly or at least quarterly statements. This should list all income and categories of spending. Any accountant can set up a good grid. It should include the following columns. First would be the targeted amount or budget for the year for each category. Second would be the actual spending for the monthly needs. Third would be spending for the year to date. The income column should also be divided into income expected for the year, actual income for the month, and actual income for the year to date. The totals for the month should enable an easy comparison of income and expenditures both for the month and for the year to date.

This income and expenditure sheet should be examined by the treasurer, who should alert the board of any aberrations. It is his job to see that spending aligns with the goals set for the budgeted year. The budget committee may work with the elders on setting the income and spending goals. A budget is a realistic faith statement. It is what we believe the LORD to provide for the coming year. When set, it can be presented to the congregation to inspire their giving. Congregational spending reflects where its vision and purposes are. Congregational members should know what they are giving toward. We believe posting monthly statements for all to see is a good policy.

We include here a Beth Messiah budget sheet. It is very detailed and is probably beyond the categories that most will need. In the early stages of congregational life, the categories of spending are much fewer. Though this is a budget from years ago, it is still very much what a budget would be like today. Do note changes in amounts for inflation. You should also note that the senior pastor on this budget was half time due to his traveling responsibilities for the network of our congregations. Otherwise it would have been double.

BETH MESSIAH CONGREGATIONAL BUDGET
(Past due from 1991 – $8,056)

		Initial 1991	Proposed 1992
1	Senior Pastor	32,226	33,384
	Salary & Housing	22,080	23,184
	Benefits	10,146	10,200
2	Minister of Evangelism	45,926	19,600
	Salary & Housing	39,736	16,000
	Benefits	6,190	3,600
3	Minister of Pastoral Care	44,387	46,477
	Salary & Housing	36,454	38,277
	Benefits	7,933	8,200
4	Music Director	18,000	18,900
5	Youth Minister	4,000	0
6	Office Staff	28,000	29,400
7	Benefits	2,500	2,500
8	Worship	3,000	3,000
9	Outreach	15,600	15,600
10	Shaliach UMJC, Benevolences, Tikkun Tuition aid, etc.	54,000	83,833
11	Tsedaka	500	500

12	Shabbat School	1,500	1,500
13	Teens Ministry	750	750
14	Home Group Ministry	300	300
15	Singles	200	200
16	Women's Ministry	200	200
17	Oneg	1500	0
18	Social Action	150	150
19	Pastor's Education	200	200
20	Education & Library	200	200
21	Shabbat Set-up	100	100
22	Prof. Consultant	2,500	2,500
23	Office Expenses	9,500	9,500
24	Newsletter	2,000	2,000
25	Rents	24,600	25,800
26	Facility	3,000	3,000
27	Utilities	1,800	1,800
28	Telephone	9,000	9,000
29	Phone System	2,400	2,400
30	Vehicle	2,000	2,000
31	Copier	3,000	0
32	Moving & Storage	2,000	2,000
33	Conferences	2,500	2,500
34	Equipment	1,500	1,500
35	Pastor's Expense	900	900
36	Fixtures-Furnishings	1,000	1,000
	Total Annual Budget	320,939	322,694
			(6,206/week)

Where Do We Spend Our Money – What is Right?

In the light of the scandals of mismanagement and ministers who live in sumptuous wealth, what is right for the minister of the LORD to make? In the early stages of congregational life, the congregation will seek to provide an adequate income for its spiritual leadership family. This means that the proportions for his salary, housing, and benefits may even be 70% or more of the total budget. The other percent will be basic office rent and rental costs for meetings and necessary communication vehicles. We do believe it is well to give 10% off the top for apostolic ministry and missions from the very start. We cannot prove this, but it fits a Scriptural pattern. The Levites received 10% and gave 10% to the priests' support. (Actually the support system was more complicated and was a larger proportion than 10% for everything.) It is well, however, to begin the faith step of regular giving in spite of immediate needs. As congregations grow, the pressure for inside needs and staff multiplies. It will never be easy to give the larger sum that 10% will represent later. When the congregation is larger, a greater amount will be given to apostolic ministry and expansion. Indeed, this should be a goal and be seen as the way of blessing. At Beth Messiah, over 25% of the budget was given to outside ministry.

Percentage Systems

Asher Intrater argues for a percentage system from day one of planting and holds to the idea that when there is adequate money in the percentages, the amount taken for staff is greater and the staff expands. Perhaps it will be 35% for staff, 20% for outreach, 20% for missions and apostolic ministry, and the rest for rental, office, and congregational needs. If a person goes the percent route, the percentages should be chosen after much prayer. Where does the LORD want us to spend? What does He want us to believe for per income? These are the standard questions for which hearing from the LORD is important. Of course, rents and bills to businesses have to be paid first as fixed costs.

It is important to be conservative in spending. If there is insufficient income in any month, the spending needs to be adjusted. Rent usually must be paid, so must the 10% tithe if there is such conviction. However, many areas can be cut. We can pray for a better month to make it up. Several months in arrears should cause a revision of the budget. By the Intrater percentage system, a congregation will never go into debt. This can also be accomplished by revising spending on short months and revising the budget if there is a period of shortfall. A congregation should never go into debt except for reasonable facility mortgages and office equipment. Furthermore, those who pay the bills – whether the pastor, the administrator, the treasurer – should anticipate large annual outlays and not be deluded into spending what is in the bank. The budget tells us what to spend, not the account balance. For example, insurance payments sometimes come annually. It is also good to have a reserve fund by including savings in the percentage.

The Leader's Salary

Full time ministers work for the Kingdom of God. It is a great privilege to work full time in the ministry. However, we must note two opposite errors in the Body. Some believe that because they are the LORD's royal children, they should live high off the hog. Since hogs are not kosher, I beg to differ. Those who hold this philosophy believe that the leader of a large ministry should be paid like a corporate executive, commensurate to their responsibility. Million dollar salaries are not unknown in the Body. This causes great stumbling since it gives more than just the appearance of profiting from the gospel. If the minister's heart is right, why would he want to be given so much for his private wealth? I personally do not care if a businessman has a mansion, if he gives the greatest portion of his income to the Kingdom. However, a minister should have a testimony of trusting the LORD for provision and not laying up treasures on earth. The examples of the apostles and first century ministers who were closest to Yeshua are a full and adequate testimony against this position.

The opposite position is equally foolish – it is to pay the minister a poverty salary! This causes undue concern for finances, and too much of his faith energy has to be used for his family's provisions. Furthermore, it will not endear the children to the ministry if ministry meant scarcity and deprivation growing up. There is no vow of poverty in the Scriptures for ministers. Shame comes on the congregation that begrudges a minister a good salary. The worker is worthy of his wages, and the elders that teach the Scriptures should receive double honor according to the Scriptures.

Our standard has been that ministers at all levels should be paid what is necessary for their living in the geographical area to which they are called to minister. This means the payment for an adequate size house, transportation, a saving plan for his children's education, health care, and a retirement plan. This is a hefty chunk, but how can we defend doing less? It is fine to give some greater remuneration for the more experienced senior person who carries a greater weight of responsibility. However, the spread should not be such that the senior man is growing rich while the junior man is hurting. Ministers need to be taught how to handle personal finances with diligence. Cost of living studies are available in most regions to enable an eldership to come to the right standards for their area.

We seek to pay other staff both according to their need and according to their abilities. Some will want to give hours voluntarily because their spouse makes a good income. The greater extent to which a congregation can run on volunteers the better.

Part of congregational financial prosperity is teaching the principles of tithing and faith giving as outlined in the Scriptures, where 1 Corinthians 9, Philippians 4, Matthew 6, Luke 6, and other passages are crucial. It is only when people take steps of faith toward the LORD in the financial realm that they enter the supernatural provision of the LORD. We teach that we give our way out of poverty and scarcity.

Insurance

It is important that congregations carry liability insurance. This covers suits from accidents on the premises of the congregation, ministerial protection from those who would sue for wrong counsel, or other real or imagined injuries. The expense is minimal and can protect the congregation from unscrupulous people whom the leaders seek to help. These types of insurance can be obtained as a rider on building fire and theft insurance.

Minister out of Relationships

We have found that a great deal of energy can be saved if people who handle an area of ministry responsibility are genuinely called to it. They will have relational commonalities with those they work with. For example, young mothers will often gravitate together for fellowship and mutual encouragement. They will be burdened for a quality nursery program. Some of them will be the coordination group for this ministry. Others with real interest and skills might join in this as well, for example, singles that gravitate to young children.

Musicians who love to worship will often come together in friendship and in mutual interest to oversee the worship under the worship leader and the pastor. Quality relationships among those who work together in an area of responsibility will greatly enhance the joy of serving. Therefore, it is a good rule of thumb to not be impatient in organizing committees and artificially joining people together. Pray about the needs of people in a specific area of service. Then make the need known. Encourage people who are interested to come together with a leader. If they have friendships and mutual concerns, this is all the better. Allow ministry committees to develop naturally.

At Beth Messiah, the elders no longer sponsor a committee night. We are not saying we never will. However, we have found that if there is a coordinator for every area that reports to the elders or deacons, and if people have a genuine interest and are responsible, they will meet as often as necessary. A responsible coordinator with responsible people will do more than a stated committee evening will produce! Therefore, allow these ministry groups to develop naturally.

CHAPTER 5

Authority, Submission, and Accountability

Accountability depends on true friendship relationships in its highest manifestation. For example, we may be accountable to the tax authorities of the Internal Revenue Service, but this is a lower level of accountability. The highest accountability is before the LORD who is our dearest friend, Father, and King. Abraham walked with the LORD, and the LORD called Abraham His friend. Many think that accountability should not be with friends because friends will not correct, rebuke, and discipline. However, this is contrary to the Scriptural ideal. The Scriptures say, "Faithful are the wounds of a friend" (Proverbs 27:6). Jesus built the twelve disciples into friendship and accountability, and He was their dearest friend. True friendship will not let the other get away with falsehood, but presses the one loved into integrity. True, it may be well to have other checks of accountability that are not based on friendship, as the auditor helps us keep the books straight. There are other possible associations one can join based on agreed upon principles that could be helpful. But, only a true friend who has built a bridge of trust into the life of the other can speak concerning the deepest issues of his life. This is "agape" love, not mere human sentiment.

In his book *Covenant Relationships*, Asher (Keith) Intrater develops our view of this. A superficial friendship that only allows the other to enter in to a limited degree prevents the intimacy of true exposure and the pain of hard but loving rebuke. Insecure leaders will avoid this kind of friendship. They will keep all at a distance. They will seek followers but not true friends. Indeed, they will not submit themselves to a plurality of friends for correction and even discipline. Even the leader of a plurality of his friends is accountable to these friends. A true plurality of leaders under a head leader to whom he is accountable is not a plurality of "yes-men." "Yes-men" could never provide the true friendship and correction that the leader needs and should want.

It cannot be too strongly stated. A leader never outgrows the need and responsibility to be accountable to a plurality of other human leaders who can remove him if he is found in disqualifying sin. It is well for every leader of a congregation to have accountability to the peers that he leads and to a body of peers who are colleagues who may give leadership to him.

Lines of Accountability

I have several lines of such accountability. First is the plurality of elders in our congregation. Second is a fellowship of pastors in our county who are mutually accountable. Third is a council of Messianic Jewish leaders from the Washington-Baltimore region. In all these cases, we meet monthly or more. Lastly, we are accountable to a national fellowship of congregations tied together through their leaders called the Union of Messianic Jewish Congregations. If one plane of accountability fails there are several others. Often it is well to ask the question, who has the legal authority to remove a leader if he falls into sin? Legal authority is often a key test to see if the accountability is real or merely a profession. In our case, the legal authority which can remove the leader is primarily in our elders and council of Messianic pastors. However, our Union and Pastors' fellowship could remove us from these organizations if we did not follow discipline. They could make our continuation in ministry difficult, though they do not have the same legal authority as the council and our elders.

Accountability may be thus provided by local pastors, an apostolic flow of congregations, a denomination or association, and a council or presbytery in a local area. Why is this so important? It is because leaders can greatly harm the sheep. A fallen, hurting leader is a dangerous leader. His wisdom cannot be trusted. May we desire to be accountable in this way so that we never hurt the sheep!

Because accountability depends on friendship, there should be true life sharing in small groups of peers. Again, the Methodist questions are good sources of accountability. We ask, "How is your spiritual and devotional life? Are you victorious over sin? How is your life of witness to the lost? How is your family life?" By sharing in this way, accountability becomes part of our lives before sin can take root. Problems are dealt with quickly. We can often thereby prevent the need to remove a leader. Such problems as marriage struggles, weariness, difficulty in child rearing, and failures in dealing with priorities can be caught. The problems can be handled quickly before they lead to gross sin.

The Extent and Limits of Authority and Submission

Members of a congregation are also called to be accountable. They are accountable to each other in small group sharing contexts under a leader. However, in the congregational setting, they are ultimately accountable to the plurality of elders. Beyond this, they are accountable to the LORD Himself. All people according to New Covenant teaching are called to build congregational community under the authority of a legitimate eldership that is defined by 1 Timothy 3 and Titus 1 standards. Elders cannot be self-appointed, but in my view they should be appointed by other elders (apostles and prophets can be a key part of this elder appointment) and affirmed by the congregational community. There is no example of self-appointment in the Scriptures, nor the idea that an elder can become one because he claims "the LORD told him" or "the LORD appointed him." Elders vet candidates for eldership and seek to prove their character qualifications and to see that their ministry already shows their call to eldership oversight, ministry, and government.

A mature, secure leader will develop structures of balanced accountability. Balance is defined by Scriptural norms. However, an insecure leader can work around even the right structure to abuse sheep. The right structure is helpful and is a safeguard, yet the right structure is less important than the character and wisdom of the leader.

We have seen members of the Body swing between over-lordship and anarchy. Because many charismatics are in rebellion to denominations, they cannot receive the wisdom of the heritage of these denominations. Therefore, the swings between over-lordship and anarchy are especially severe. Because charismatics are unclear as to the training requirements for leaders, they have allowed many unqualified and insecure men and women to come into leadership. This has produced tremendous pain and destruction in the lives of people.

What is proper authority? Proper authority seeks to raise mature disciples who are dependent on leadership but become dependent on the LORD. Members should embrace a voluntary interdependence for the sake of the Kingdom because our gifts alone are not adequate for the work of the LORD. Teamwork, mutual accountability, and recognition of differing gifts are crucial for the work of the Kingdom. The LORD has set it up so we will forever need each other to do His work. However, it will not be in an immature dependency. Our full potential can only be realized in groups where we all give and receive in the gifts of the Holy Spirit through each other. True leaders want to reproduce leaders and want others to be released into leadership.

Insecure leaders want to protect their unique role in leadership and to see that all others remain followers.

In the life of the congregation, the leaders have the right to set direction for the congregation. If a specific leadership direction is foundational and members cannot eventually come to agree with it, they will have to find a community more in accord with their vision. However, true vision comes from the LORD through the leaders to the people. The people are not called to set the vision and direction. The people are called to follow if they can affirm the vision. It is important as well that leaders have the right to place people in positions of responsibility and remove them. They alone have the full knowledge of the person's life and their quality of performance. People must give leaders some trust to do this and not second-guess every decision. Some covenantal humility is required of the people to enable the leaders to lead with greater joy.

The Call of Leaders and Submission and Obedience

Leaders are called to correct, rebuke, exhort, and teach. People are called to be receptive to correction – to be teachable. Leaders have the authority to enforce the standards of the LORD in the community. Whatever the Scripture requires, they may require. However, over-lordship does not recognize the crucial limit of authority. That limit is seen in the fact that any member of the Body may go directly before the head, Yeshua. In the army, the general commands the lesser officers who command the troops. So in the Scriptures there are leaders of tens, hundreds, and thousands – yet there is a major difference. Every person in the New Covenant has complete access at all times to the General Himself. The lowliest new member has the potential to hear the voice of the LORD directly.

A true leader embraces the dynamic tension of seeking to have members embrace the congregational vision while also seeking to train his members to directly hear the voice of the LORD. Each person has the Holy Spirit within. Therefore, if they follow, it will be by affirming the vision through the Spirit. It will not be by fear, intimidation, or other forms of manipulation. Because everyone has the Spirit, we must allow for the awesome – and yet sometimes messy – results of people following their own consciences before the LORD. If what a person believes to be the will of the LORD by the Spirit goes contrary to leadership advice for his personal life direction, he must follow his conviction. We can only limit a person's freedom to follow his conscience before the Spirit by the teaching of the Scriptures. Whatever is contrary to the Scriptures is never the word of the Spirit. True Scriptural leadership will affirm this right of conscience before the LORD. The call to submission entails obedience to authority where it is in accord with the Scriptures.

We believe in making a distinction between affirmation and confirmation. In confirmation, the leaders and friends of a person agree with their sense of direction for their own lives. When a person makes major life direction decisions, they should include their closest friends and leaders in the process. However, this process is one of advice and counsel. It must not be so heavy that it blunts the potential of a person hearing the LORD. Those making life directional decisions should understand that their decisions will affect the whole Body. No man is an island. Therefore it is only right to include others – it is the way of love. If the others confirm the decision, the person will have the boost of faith agreement from his fellows. Perhaps there will even be prophecy to confirm. If such confirmation in the Spirit (which does strengthen resolve especially if accompanied by supernatural prophecy) is not forthcoming, the person must go before the LORD again. If the conviction remains, he must follow the LORD's leading. There is no power in a guilty or suppressed conscience. In a case such as this, we should recognize the right to conscience and be supportive even if we disagree. There must be no social ostracism for making decisions contrary to leadership advice and counsel. Such ostracism is the beginning of manipulation, and subtle cultic control begins here.

This brings us to a significant problem. The immature or carnal person may make major decisions poorly and repeatedly. This is especially a problem when the head of a family does so. There is much teaching in charismatic circles that when one hears the voice of the LORD, they are to ask no man. However, how many have such an accuracy of hearing? Only the most mature can follow such advice. Indeed, even the most mature sometimes miss it. The voice of the LORD does not always come with such clarity on the receiving end, even to the mature. The process of accountability and confirmation is a safeguard against terribly flaky decisions. What is leadership to do about the present issue? First, they can confront the sin patterns and carnality in a person's life and point out how they are the foundation for bad decisions. Secondly, they can point out the results of the many bad decisions made under the claim, "The LORD told me." The LORD speaks with those who are solid in their fellowship and responsibility toward Him and others. Spiritual and mature people do hear the LORD with significant accuracy. This should be taught. At Beth Messiah, the more mature did not use the language, "The LORD told me." We discouraged it. It can be a manipulative way to remove others input into decisions and avoiding the confirmation process. Having said all this, however, we must still allow even the flaky to follow their conscience. Perhaps they will only learn through the school of hard knocks. We can point out that there must be something wrong when wise counsel is refused again and again. "Are mature leaders never in accord with my personal life decisions? Why?" These are questions to be explored, but the right of decision before the LORD in good conscience is still the right of even the most immature adult.

Confirmation is a great safeguard against rash decisions. Affirmation is a great safeguard to individual conscience, including allowing a person to make contrary decisions preserving individual conscience. To truly affirm may mean even to give a party to the one who leaves town against leadership counsel. It means to be open to continuing relationships.

What I am saying here will not satisfy the independent type who will reject the nature of confirmation and the corporate nature of spiritual life. It also will not satisfy the leaders who feel they must do something to prevent the unwise decisions of sheep and make them conform to counsel. I believe both are wrong responses. What can we do? We can pray for the person. We can point out the truth of their lack of receiving wise counsel. We can encourage them to commit to a quality devotional life with the LORD. If they are consistent here, they will change. If a head of household does foolish things to cause his family suffering by making decisions for foolish schemes ("The LORD told me to enter this business deal"), we can ultimately enjoin congregational discipline. Scripture does allow discipline for irresponsibility in not providing for the family. Such a man is said to be "worse than an infidel" (1 Timothy 5:8). We must not use congregational funds to bail him out. We also must not violate the principle of decision making in conscience. However, in a severe case of irresponsibility, we can say, "Bill, you will seek to get a regular stable job with a salary or risk being disfellowshipped from this congregation." In such a situation, there should be a long enough track record of irresponsibility that the discipline would be affirmed by most of the people who believe in discipline.

Input from the Congregational Family

Although the elders are the final decision making body, they are wise to respect the input of the membership. Wise elders will seriously consider changing directions if the people do not confirm the new direction. The people should have input in the choosing of elders and deacons. The elders prayerfully choose an elder or deacon, usually one who is already moving in a pattern of ministry that foreshadows the office, and then they announce their nominee and wait for input. A significant period (at least a month) should elapse before the elder or deacon nominee is finally installed with the laying on of hands. During this time, the elders need to gauge the sense of the congregation. Do they receive the person in this new role?

The congregational meeting can be a good time for coordinators in every area to make reports and receive input (evangelism, education, nursery, cell groups, worship, social action etc.). Running a congregational meeting requires a leader's willingness to enforce Ephesians 4:25-5:2. No evil talk or bitterness will be allowed in expression, but only such as is good for edification. Positive and corrective criticism is allowed if brought in a spirit of love and trust. These meetings can be a joy and have been at Beth Messiah for many years.

When a congregation grows large, the annual congregational meeting will become too large for adequate input. Reports can be made at these meetings, but the home cell structure will be the best source of feedback. The cells over which an elder nominee serves can give the best input on his nomination. Cell members may also best know the one who will serve as a deacon. The issues of the congregation can be discussed in a cell meeting. The elders can then receive this information from the cell leaders. These are ways to keep the life of the congregation open.

There can be a wonderful unity of purpose if the congregational core trusts its leaders, the leaders respect the people, and there is a good quality of spiritual life in the community.

CHAPTER 6

Discipline in Congregational Life

The elders are responsible for enforcing the LORD's basic standards in congregational life. The background for understanding the function of elders is in the Hebrew Scriptures. Therein we read of the responsibility of the elders – or judges at the gate – to render decisions in disputes, to enforce the laws of the LORD, and to give wise counsel. The description of eldership qualifications and responsibilities in 1 Timothy 3 and Titus 1 make it clear that the elders of New Covenant congregations perform parallel functions. (See my book entitled *Due Process*.)

Fulfilling Standards

The Scriptures require fulfilling Scriptural standards for both leaders and members. When leaders fail to fulfill Scriptural leadership standards, they must be removed from leadership until they re-qualify. They now become members like other members of the congregation. When members fail to fulfill basic membership standards, they may become members "not in good standing" or may even be ultimately disfellowshipped if there is serious sin. However, the first concern of the elders when a member fails to fulfill membership standards is to restore the member. Love is the motive. The second concern is to see that disrepute is not brought on the name of Yeshua because of people who profess to be His followers but live contrary to the Scriptures. The final concern is to see that the sheep are protected from either false professors or those who are in deception. All these concerns are part of the call of the elders to see that New Covenant communities are expressions of love and justice. We read of the Messiah Yeshua, "He will not rest or be discouraged until He has established justice on the earth, and the nations will seek after His law." How is it that He seeks to establish this? It is through His people. It begins with our communities being congregations where His Kingdom rule is maintained, where love and justice are in manifestation. In the Age to Come, Messiah will not be seeking to establish justice. He will have established it and will be maintaining it! He works for this justice through His people and their work of extending the Kingdom in declaring the Good News.

Establishing Love and Justice

Love and justice are only possible in a community when elders take up their responsibility to establish love and justice by the power of the Spirit working in and through them. Furthermore, love and justice can only be established when the Scriptural standards of due process are followed in congregational discipline matters. It is my belief that no one should be an elder, and certainly not a congregational leader or planter, without understanding their responsibilities to establish the LORD's order of justice and love in congregational life. The leader must be apt to teach covenant responsibilities applied to the way we handle difficulties with brothers and sisters. He must know how to prevent unholy factions from forming by people sharing their offenses and hurts in destructive ways. Rumor, gossip, and slander are common in the world, but must be precluded in the life of a congregation. Yet all of this must be done without falling into over-lordship control over people. The Scriptural process of handling disputes, conflicts, and offenses is the way for the LORD's order to be enforced. I will only give a brief summary here, as I have written an entire book on this entitled *Due Process*, and my colleague Michael Rudolph has written a few works.[4] However, I urge the reader to know the content of these books. Also, Asher Intrater's *Covenant Relationships* is an important manual.

Formal Membership

In our American constitutional and legal system, formal membership is very important. Formal membership is the official covenanting of people to the congregation and the leaders. In formal membership, the person declares his intention to live according to Scriptural standards in the community of faith. He professes to understand his responsibilities and rights as a member under the leadership of a specific congregation's elders. He also professes to be subject to the principles of congregational discipline. My book *Growing to Maturity* is our manual for this commitment. American courts have upheld the right of congregational discipline repeatedly, but only when there is a clearly understood formal membership covenant entered by the party. Without such a covenant, congregations have been sued successfully for invasion of privacy when they carry out Scriptural discipline.

In our anti-formal and anti-authority society, there will always be people who will claim that formal membership was not in the Scriptures. However, I believe it most certainly was. Covenant immersion (baptism) was understood as a legal act before witnesses. It subjected the convert to Judaism and to the government of Israel. In the same way, in the New Covenant, it subjected the person to the government of the community in the locality where the person resided. There were exceptions, but New Testament baptism usually took place before witnesses and was a legally binding act. People in the first century understood this well. The New Covenant Scriptures did not have to elaborate. The baptized person submitted under the eldership of the city in which they resided.

At Beth Messiah Congregation and now in other Tikkun congregations, the candidates for immersion were given instruction by which they understood this covenant. They then become formal provisional members. They will be under the jurisdiction of the elders of Beth Messiah until they either transfer to another congregation or progress to become full formal members of Beth Messiah after finishing the *Growing to Maturity* course. Provisional membership is also a category for transfers from other congregations until they complete *Growing to Maturity*. We seek to avoid having members of the Body in our midst that see Beth Messiah Congregation as their congregation, yet they have no clear submission to the jurisdiction of the elders. If a provisional member of Beth Messiah decides that Beth Messiah is not the place where they are called, we will do our best to help them find a Scripturally based congregation where they are called.

Therefore, there were two ways to become a member of Beth Messiah. One was by immersion. The other is by a legitimate transfer from another congregation. The steps to full membership enable a person to make sure they are truly called here and are in accord with the vision of the congregation. The *Growing to Maturity* course helps a person to clarify this. This was the classical standard in Protestantism.

Members are expected to fulfill basic standards of righteous living and congregational participation. If participation becomes inadequate, they are not disfellowshipped. This is reserved for those who commit gross sin and do not repent. Rather, the person who fails to fulfill involvement standards becomes a member not in good standing. They can be transferred to another congregation in such a situation, but their status as such would be made known to the new pastor or eldership. A member not in good standing is under the discipline of being exhorted but fellowship is offered to draw the person into the community. When a person is disfellowshipped for gross sin, fellowship is withheld until there is repentance. Therefore, there are four kinds of membership status: a provisional member in good standing, a provisional member not in good standing, a full member in good standing, and a full member not in good standing. A person who is disfellowshipped is not a member.

It is important to note that in many countries the legal benefits of the United States are not available. I still believe that a written covenant of membership is a very good thing so that people know what they are buying into. This protects all involved, and people then have a choice with full disclosure and no hidden agendas. Such a document of understanding only takes a page or two. I also believe it is good for a congregation to have a governing document so that all members know the decision making process, their responsibilities, and the responsibilities of leaders.

Due Process in Congregational Life

The elders of a congregation are like the elders of the gate in the towns in ancient Israel. As such, they must see to it that those who are allowed in the city are not destructive to the city or the congregation. The elders need to teach the principles of due process found in the Scriptures. Matthew 16 is a good starting point for this teaching. In this passage Peter declares the following to Yeshua, "You are the Messiah, the Son of the living God." Jesus responded to him by declaring that He was giving him the keys to the Kingdom of Heaven and whatever he bound on earth was bound in heaven. The rabbis of the Talmudic period believed that they had these keys and the right to bind and to loose. They believed it was transferred from the ancient priests and judges to them. The Sanhedrin was the Jewish high court in the days of Yeshua. What were the keys? The keys were the rights of government and judicial authority in ancient

Israel. When Yeshua transferred the keys from the Sanhedrin to the apostles in Matthew 16 and 18, He gave them the highest judicial authority in the Body. They would also be the leading judges in the Age to Come. Its application is the authority of elders over the communities of faith that Yeshua established. To bind and loose meant the right to forbid behavior (bind) and to permit behavior (loose). The terminology is judicial and unmistakable in its first century Jewish context. Remember, here was a band of Jewish disciples who believed that Yeshua was the Messiah, which means the ruler King of Israel destined to sit on David's throne. He is the chief Judge, High Priest, and King. Therefore, the confession of His Messiah-ship was the fitting time to declare the position of the disciples as the judges and rulers under Him. The disciples still had to learn what this would mean for a transitional age where the Kingdom would not come in fullness. However, the words of Yeshua were unmistakable for them. They would be the rulers to settle disputes, to enforce the law of the LORD, and to apply that law to new situations in binding and loosing.

Matthew 18:15 carries this theme further. It is a key passage concerning the standards of covenant love to be enjoined upon the community of faith. It is also the foundational guide for the elders or judges of the new community of New Covenant faith. All readers should be careful to study this chapter. Here is an outline of the key points.

1) Disciples of Jesus should seek to settle their disputes by having the love and courage to confront each other. This confrontation is to be in private between the parties involved. It is not to be spread to others. There is to be no gutless gossip. If the brother or sister repents of sin, that is the end of the matter. Other passages make it clear that if a leader is in sin, there is an exception. Because the leader in serious sin becomes disqualified, it will be necessary for the situation to be confessed to the elders. This passage makes

it clear that we are our brother's keepers. All members are to be responsible for exhorting one another to repentance and righteousness. The nature of community life requires that this not be done over every little thing. "Love will cover a multitude of sins" (Proverbs 10:12, 1 Peter 4:8). There will be many minor offenses. We must not be super sensitive or we will have no time for anything other than confrontation meetings. However, when significant sin is involved, it is our responsibility to bring correction.

2) When the brother or sister refuses to repent, two or three others are to be brought into the process of confrontation. If the truth is admitted, they become witnesses to the situation. If they were a direct witness of the sin, the confrontation is all the more powerful. Matthew 18 is the briefest summary of due process. Therefore it does not cover all of the situations. A person may deny their sin or be wrongly confronted. The situation may be a case of one person's word against another. In this scenario, the person who is wronged only has recourse to prayer and to self-crucifying silence, being sure that the LORD will eventually reveal the truth. Where there are two or three witnesses, the person may repent. If they truly repent, which in Scriptural terms includes the proof of repentance by making restitution where appropriate, the matter should go no further. We are not to destroy trust for the person in the community of faith. Restitution may be monetary, or it may be restoring the reputation of the one who was slandered by going to those who were given bad reports.

3) Where the person does not repent and there are two or three witnesses, the situation is to be told to the congregation. There is disagreement on how to interpret this. There are pro's and con's for each position. Some believe that this means to tell it to the elders as the leaders of the congregation. Others believe that the witnesses tell the congregation

about their confrontation – with the elders present. Then the congregation under its elders would exhort the person to repent. This assumes Jewish first century standards for courts where the elders may judge the evidence – and the accused have a right of defense before the judges. Again, all of this is not brought out here but is clear from other passages such as 1 Corinthians 6.

4) If the person will not listen to the congregation and its elders, he is to no longer be considered part of the community of faith. In other words, the person is to be disfellowshipped. Such a person is compared to a tax collector or pagan who is outside the community. This is very important. A person must not be allowed to discredit the good news of the Kingdom by claiming to be a member of the Body while remaining in unrepentance regarding gross sin. The good news of the Kingdom is deliverance from gross sin. Yeshua does enjoin us to forgive "seventy times seven." However, this forgiveness does not imply that a person who continually falls into gross sin may not be put under stricter discipline and accountability before the community to test their repentance.

Kingdom Authority

In the parable of the vineyard, similar to Matthew 16 and 18, Yeshua transfers the authority of the Kingdom from the Sanhedrin to the apostles and those who follow them (Matthew 21). In Acts 15 we see the Apostles and elders exercising their authority to bind and loose. Gentiles are loosed from the calling to live a Jewish life – but not from the moral norms of the Torah. They are bound as for living righteously in Yeshua.

The question naturally arises: "What makes up gross sin or doctrinal error by which a person should be disfellowshipped?

Classical Evangelicalism's universally held doctrinal positions are valid standards in judging doctrine. In the New Testament we find catalogues of sins that, if they are practiced, preclude a person from entering the Kingdom of God. The local Body is a manifestation of that Kingdom. One of the catalogues of gross sins, in 1 Corinthians 5:11, enjoins us to have nothing to do with a person who practices gross sins. A study of this issue will show that sins which required the penalty of death or exile in the Hebrew Scriptures require disfellowshipping from the congregations of the New Covenant.

The Call for New Covenant Courts

In 1 Corinthians 6 we read about the call to the Corinthian congregation to settle disputes under judges in their community. They are not to bring disputes between brothers to the courts of the world. The meaning of the term elder should alert us to the fact that elders are to enforce Scriptural standards and form a judicial bar in every congregation. Acts 15 gives us the example of a court of appeal for cases that are too destructive or difficult for the local eldership. The government of the New Covenant communities looks amazingly like the government of Israel during the period of the judges before there was one king. New Covenant congregational government cannot enjoin corporal punishments, but its sanctions are very important nonetheless.

The importance of teaching these things to the congregation cannot be overstated. A congregation that is not taught these things will not support congregational discipline. They will misinterpret it as harsh rather than as the LORD's way to bring repentance. Humanistic mercy often exalts itself against the teaching of the Scriptures. Therefore we seek to disciple every new member in these principles.

When Covenant Principles are Violated

Frequently today in congregational life, covenant principles are violated. The violation of covenant principles is serious sin since it destroys the fabric of community. The LORD says that He will severely judge those who destroy a congregation since it is a temple or dwelling place for the Spirit of the LORD (1 Corinthians 3:16-19). There is often little loyalty in building stable communities, and people will frequently change congregations without much thought. In addition, when people are offended by a member or a leader, they will often spread their offense to others outside the bounds of covenantal righteousness. Members take up offenses for the one who improperly shares. Sometimes members have grounds for their offenses against members and leaders. Sometimes those offended (at times without grounds) at leaders find others who are also offended at them. The ones so offended with those who take up offenses find each other in a fellowship of mutual offense. Sometimes those who are disgruntled, but not offended at the same people, join the faction. The only thing they have in common is that they have offenses. When this happens, the congregation is in a mode toward destruction. If the faction is significant in size, I recommend calling on outside leaders to help.

Lest I am misunderstood, I want to make it clear that leaders who violate Scriptural principles and exercise over-lordship have to repent and in severe cases may have to step down. There should be a court of appeal concerning a leader who exercises tyranny. However, rebellious members will often claim tyranny when there is none.

When this happens, a board of elders must call for the people who have formed such a faction to repent. They can only do this by teaching the Scriptures unless witnesses will come forward and testify of the covenantal violation. All who broke Matthew 18 standards must be enjoined to go back and follow the right processes for their grievances and repent for improper sharing. However, because the accusations were spread, the elders who will be called to judge the situation must make their findings known to all who were improperly drawn in and clear the air.

For three examples of how to handle factions, see Appendix II. What questions should be asked? Often those who form factions enter a demonic sphere of influence. The action they desire would destroy the community, but they are not conscious of it. Those who are so given to evil spirits demand that leaders be removed although they cannot prove their accusations in the mouth of two or three witnesses.

In all of this, an important principle should be stated. Although prophetic ability may help a leader discern who to place in leadership and may give wisdom, discipline must be based on empirical evidence in the mouth of two or three witnesses. Prophetic discernment is not the proof of wrong doing. This is the standard for accusations against members and, as Paul notes, is the standard for receiving reports against elders.

Liability insurance, which was recommended in the last chapter, can be a protection for the congregation which enforces discipline. Those given to evil can sue a congregation for legitimate discipline. However, since our society recognizes the authority of congregational discipline, this is a court battle worthy to be fought.

We trust that this section on discipline will be helpful to you. Please do refer to the other materials recommended in this chapter.

Dealing with Problem People

The phrase "problem people" is used in the writings of Ralph Neighbor. Dudley Hall speaks of people who are high maintenance and low output. In a Messianic Jewish congregation, these may be larger challenges than the ordinary. Every congregation needs to deal with the dysfunctional aspects of people. However, through repentance and the inner healing power of the cross and the resurrection, a person should come to a fruitful, joyful life in a brief period, perhaps within a year or two of discipling. Of course, we are "being saved" and will be "being healed" all our lives.

Before speaking of specific Messianic Jewish challenges, I do want to speak of a particular pattern that is likely to be present today. Within the followers of Yeshua, metaphors have developed to describe problem patterns. One such metaphor that is common today is the Jezebel-Ahab metaphor. Jezebel was Queen during the days of King Ahab in ancient Israel. The accounts can lead us to believe that Jezebel was the stronger person in the relationship. She certainly had great power in ancient Israel. Elijah fled at the threat of Jezebel, not Ahab. The book of Revelation warns against allowing Jezebel to minister in the congregation. Was this a literal woman in chapter two, or simply an individual or group like Queen Jezebel who brought immorality? This has prompted many teachers to claim that there is a Jezebel spirit that can come into a congregation through an individual or a group actually influenced by an evil spiritual power. The root of this is weak men who either abuse their families or fail to take loving servant leadership roles in their families. It is also rooted in women who seek to be in control of their families by manipulation and domination. Perhaps unhealed hurt can be at the root of the problem. The woman responds to the abuse she has experienced by seeking to be in control. Some see this as the spirit behind radical feminism.

It must be stated here that the spirit of Jezebel manifests itself in men too – not just women. A man can seek and maintain control through intimidation, manipulation, and through humiliating others who are under him. Both men and women can play the role of "seducer." A man can be manipulative as a means to gain desired goals. It is stated in Scripture that such men "creep into households and make captives of gullible women" (2 Timothy 3:6-9). The spirit of Jezebel both inspires abuse of authority and undermines the authority of others. This spirit both castrates authority and breeds mistrust and despising of authority. It perpetuates the spirit of lawlessness.

How are we to evaluate this paradigm? I do believe that this analysis can be over applied. Every marital problem and congregational problem need not be analyzed in terms of the spirit of Jezebel and Ahab. However, I do confess that many of our major conflicts in congregational life have come from people whose family lives were not in order, where a weak vacillating man was married to an un-submitted and manipulative or dominating woman. When several of these patterned families get together, they may form an awesome faction. Gossip and bad reports may be part of the mechanism of destruction. While discipline must be based on evidence and testimony, prophecy can warn us to pray. We have seen healing in unhealthy families who have been under the oppression of this pattern. But, when there is an unwillingness to deal with this pattern in a group of people, and there is not sufficient evidence to bring discipline, there still can be a strong negative influence in the community. I have seen manipulated men in such situations as well. Spiritual gifts may dry up or be replaced by false gifts. Men in spiritual authority sense a lack of spiritual power – impotence. It is as if a strong projection of negative judgments is coming from people saying, "You do not measure up; you are inept." Such mistrust is projected toward the one in authority, and often it begins to affect even the most secure leader. He begins to doubt his own authority and begins to believe that he is doing everything wrong. When he tries to bring correction, the recipient does not repent but points out that he (the leader) is not doing it in love – or not doing it exactly according to Matthew 18. The case is thrown out because of a mistrial. The focus changes and the attention shifts toward how rotten the authority is. Many leaders fall for this very subtle form of lawlessness out of their own insecurity. Confusion and discouragement often settle in. The standard for correction is no longer the Scriptures but the behavior of the leader. "I don't have to obey unless I agree with what is being said and how you are telling me. I don't have to obey unless I respect you." Indeed, the leader becomes inept if he falls for this deception!

Fasting and prayer is the proper recourse in this instance. It will bring hidden things to light. I recall one difficult period in congregational life where we sensed that this was the problem. We did not identify individuals, families, or couples. We simply fasted, prayed, and asked the LORD to break the Jezebel-Ahab spirit attacking the congregation. Within a month eight families left the congregation, some who never indicated that they were having problems in the community. We were amazed that every couple was patterned according to a weak husband and a dominating or manipulative wife. This pattern has happened in several other congregations after prayer. We have come to believe that Scriptural family order is absolutely central for congregational life. No one should be in leadership without establishing this order. After the exodus, the congregation experienced new spiritual power, growth, and confidence in the leadership!

Congregants must be trained to have faith in the LORD toward their leaders (and wives toward their husbands). It is the LORD that they are contending with and not man. All authority – both good and bad – is put into place by the LORD, and He is the one who will move upon both the just and the unjust to fulfill His purposes. Until we stop blaming one another, we will not break out of the pattern of abuse/victim retaliation, whether it involves men or women.

In Messianic Jewish congregations there is an added challenge of our not identifying with the majority cultures of the Christian community. At the same time, we take a stand for Jewishness and Jesus that was historically rejected by the Jewish community. Because of this stance, there is an onslaught by the powers of darkness who seek to preclude the reestablishment of the "saved remnant of Israel." There is a pressure to wrongly identify with Rabbinic Judaism in a legalistic way, or to become anti-Jewish in "super-spiritual" orientation. This is exacerbated by the dysfunctions of some people who take these stands. In *Growing to Maturity*, I laid out some of my concerns under the subtitle, "Four Problem Types in Messianic

Judaism." I am more convinced than ever that this analysis is correct and from the Spirit.

I noted that first we find the "super Jewish legalist." The person in this mode seeks to turn the Messianic Jewish congregation into the exact pattern of a traditional synagogue. There must be a fixed liturgy. Changes or adaptations of the traditions of our people are rejected. We may talk about Yeshua in our preaching, but the general orientation in worship is to be the unchanging pattern. We are speaking now of the extreme, yet this mind-set exists in those who are not quite so extreme. For a person of this persuasion, the manifestation of spiritual gifts or a change in the liturgy is greatly offensive. Complaints and dissatisfaction of this type produce a negative spirit in the community and are destructive of freedom.

The opposite of this person is the "anti-Jewish member." This person finds every cantorial or liturgical piece to be "unspiritual" and a diversion from "loving Jesus." This includes chanting a psalm, wearing tallit (prayer shawls) or having a Passover Seder. We have seen several sources for this stance. One explanation is self-hatred in the Jewish person as a response to past persecution that he, his family, or relatives may have received. Another factor is hatred for all things from the synagogue because of a bad experience growing up in Judaism. Still another reason is that one's salvation and early discipleship experience were in a Gentile, non-liturgical cultural context that became identified with true spirituality. Anything that does not duplicate their early experiences seems unspiritual. Perhaps it is a combination of these factors. Some in this mode believe they are called to bring the Messianic Jewish congregation to a more spiritual place where they will shed the diversions of Jewish life and culture.

We also have "super charismatic rebellious types" who will not allow their gifts and words or even their lives to be tested and refined in submission to community government. In contrast to this we have the "anti-charismatic legalist" who may theoretically accept the reality of the gifts of the Spirit but is over concerned for decorum. The Spirit's moving is not always neat. People respond in various ways. The over concern for decorum is a manifestation of the fear of man or the fear of losing control. Such a person misses the objective quality of the supernatural when it really happens! Valid and precise prophetic words of knowledge do not necessarily impress them. These folks really want a predictable service and desire to stop the public practice of spiritual gifts. Of course, one can see that the "anti-charismatic legalist" may make an alliance with the "super-Jewish Jew" if he likes Jewish expressions. However, the super charismatic rebellious may be in league with the anti-Jewish Jew.

What is the solution to these problems? First, it is crucial that the leaders come to unity about their vision and how the various aspects of it are to fit together. They must clearly and regularly put forth the vision. Regularly putting forth clear vision is one key to unity. Some will complain about the repetition of the vision, but it is essential. This will influence people to leave who are not in accord with the vision. They need to become convinced that they are not going to change the vision of the leadership. Besides speaking the vision, personal counsel may bring others past their hang-ups and into greater accord. The leaders must not tolerate people in their ranks who undercut their vision. If they spread disunity, the basic standards of discipline should be enjoined. When there are those in your midst, especially leaders, who are promoting their own vision rather than bringing their vision under the head pastor's or community vision, they will scatter the sheep instead of gathering them. Putting forth vision and counsel, and doing confrontation well, is the basic way to handle these problems. By the way, these problems can be integrated with other personal problems like the Ahab-Jezebel syndrome. Seek the Spirit's wisdom on how to go on.

CHAPTER 7

Signs and Wonders and Growth

The gifts of the Spirit are keys to the work of the LORD. On the cutting edge of proclaiming the Good News of the Kingdom, signs and wonders are important instruments of the Spirit. Gifts of the Spirit are also important for encouraging fellow members – building them up – and for bringing spiritual and physical healing on all levels of their lives. We will give a brief outline on the use of the gifts of the Spirit in four settings:

1) On the cutting edge of serving the lost or evangelism
2) In the home cell group
3) In the weekly celebration
4) In personal counseling

This is not a chapter on the nature of the gifts of the Spirit and their use in general. This is outlined in *Growing to Maturity*. There are other excellent books on this. Our task is guidance for leaders in governing.

It is crucial that leadership comes to a conviction on the essential place of the gifts of the Spirit. John Wimber uses the term "gracelets" for the gifts. These are means and manifestations from the Spirit by which He empowers us for His work through us unto the building up of the Body. The word for "gift" in the original Greek is from the same root as "grace." To think that we can carry out His work without His grace or empowerment is foolish indeed. However, the gifts may not always be seen in extraordinary manifestations. Insights and words of wisdom may be recognized as from their supernatural source, but others may miss this. It is nonetheless His gifting.

One of my sad experiences in travel is to find that many congregations that call themselves charismatic practice very little of the gifts of the Spirit. Such manifestations are not welcome or encouraged by leaders. Why? There are many reasons. There could be sin in the congregation, division, or lack of teaching, and thus lack of faith for the gifts of the Spirit. However, the primary cause in many congregations is that the leadership is not confident in their ability to govern in a context of prophetic and power gifts. Therefore, they seek to squelch the gifts even if their theology gives theoretical affirmation. We should see from the pages of the New Testament that this is not an option. Part of the essence of the New Covenant is the outpouring of the Holy Spirit. The Jewish background of the New Testament proves beyond a doubt that in the Jewish mind, the presence of the Spirit was associated with manifestations of the Spirit. The fulfillment of Joel 2:28ff at the feast of Shavuot in Acts 2 shows that manifestations or gifts of the Spirit were part of the initial outpouring. That such gifts and manifestations are a normative part of New Covenant life is proven by an unprejudiced reading of the rest of the New Testament.

The Baptism in the Holy Spirit and the Motivation for Ministry

We believe that every person is called to experience the joy of the filling of the Spirit. The first experience of this filling of the

Spirit is commonly called the baptism of the Holy Spirit. I do not believe that the baptism of the Spirit is necessarily accompanied by the gift of speaking in tongues. Baptism means immersion. Martin Lloyd Jones, in his excellent book *Joy Unspeakable*, argues that when you have been immersed in the Spirit you know it. This baptism can be manifested by joy unspeakable, by supernatural gifts, or by incredible love for the LORD and for others. I believe that it is easy for most to speak in tongues when they are filled. However, I did not receive the gift of tongues until four years after my first dramatic infilling. Being filled with the Spirit is the heritage and right of every truly born-again disciple. It is appropriated by faith. Frank Macchia has written what I consider the definitive defense of the importance of the baptism in the Spirit in his book *Baptized in the Spirit: A Global Pentecostal Theology*. It is very scholarly and convincing, and I strongly recommend it.

Mark 16:15 summarizes the belief of the early congregations of the Messiah. "These signs shall follow them that believe." The familiar list of speaking with new tongues, being protected from poison and serpents, casting out demons and healing the sick, were considered a normal part of New Covenant life. Some would question the textual validity of Mark 16:15, but it is still an important witness to the convictions held during the last part of the first century.

Ephesians 4 presents key ministry leadership people as specially gifted by the Holy Spirit as well. They equip the saints for the work of the ministry until they reach the maturity of the Messiah. Paul in Romans 12 lists the gifts of the Spirit in terms of the differences of basic ministry callings in people. People are motivated by their callings. Some like Hickey read Romans 12 as indicating that a person may have only one ministry motive gift. However, I believe that although a specific ministry gift usually predominates in every person, ministry may be motivated by different combinations of ministry gifts. Primary gifts may change over the course of a lifetime. The list of 1 Corinthians 12 has overlapping meaning with Romans 12. The verses in 1 Corinthians 12 seem to be a list of the types of manifestation that come through members of the Body. Because all true disciples have the Holy Spirit, any member of the Body may show any of the nine manifestations of the Spirit in the 1 Corinthians 12 list. In the LORD's distribution, the combinations of manifestations vary in a person to person variety.

The Motive of Love

It is important that we not judge spirituality by manifestations of the Holy Spirit. The fruit of the Spirit or righteous character traits (love, joy, peace, patience, etc.) are the key criteria for evaluating true spirituality. We are told that we shall know a true disciple by his fruit in service to others as well.

It is also important that disciples be motivated by love for others in their use of the gifts of the Spirit. Too many are motivated by pride and attention seeking. A faithful disciple desperately wants to help others or to set them free, along with desiring the power of the LORD to be effective in doing so. Love is the motive for the operation of the gifts. This is the point of 1 Corinthians 13. It is not love instead of gifts as some falsely interpret. Love is the necessary motive behind the operation of gifts. We are commanded to seek the best gifts. At the end of 1 Corinthians 12 and the beginning of 1 Corinthians 14, we read commands to desire the gifts of the Spirit for the building up of others, but it also teaches that the motive must be love (1 Corinthians 13).

Those who have moved most powerfully in the manifestations of the Spirit have warned that our quest for respectability is contrary to the anointing. There are times when the Spirit moves in such a gentle way in a well governed gathering that only the most rigid would be offended. However, at other times the manifestations of the Spirit seem offensive. John White, a leading Christian psychiatrist, has written an excellent book on this entitled *When the Spirit Comes with Power* (Inter Varsity Press). White shows that many genuine manifestations of the Holy Spirit are contrary to Emily Post standards of gracious civilized etiquette. Casting out a demon is sometimes messy as we see in the pages of the New Testament, as I learned firsthand in Chicago in the early 1970s. When people genuinely fall under the power of the Spirit (and there is much that is not genuine in this regard), it looks really flaky. Before it is harshly judged, the person who went down under the power should be interviewed and asked what happened. For some, it is an immersion in the Spirit in such power that they cannot stand. The natural eye does not see what is happening. I am not giving an apologetic that one should seek unseemly looking manifestations. These types of manifestation were the exceptions in our post message ministry at Beth Messiah, but we have come to not be embarrassed if it genuinely happens. We do correct those who seek attention by regularly repeating the pattern.

I do believe that the Holy Spirit's gifts and manifestations take place through actual cessationists, without them knowing it. Cessationists are people who deny that the gifts are for today. One famous fundamentalist teaches, with great dogmatism, the view that the gifts passed away when the perfect came (that is the Scriptures). However, a key piece of property for this ministry was obtained at a truly incredible price – after this leader had a prophecy during a prayer meeting that the owner would sell the property at this particularly ridiculous low price. In the past, he had refused to sell even above the market price. This prophecy was exactly fulfilled. Ministry leaders regularly tell this story not realizing it was a prophecy. They see it as an amazing sense in prayer!

The Importance of Learning to Govern

It is very important that governmental leaders become practiced in ministering in contexts where the gifts of the Spirit manifest. It is not necessary to be as prophetic or supernaturally endowed as the ones governed. However, the leader does need discernment and a good sense of what is going on in the contexts of the Spirit moving. Not everyone who has been filled with the Spirit can do this. Years ago I was greatly lacking in confidence in such governing. I did not know how to run meetings of the type where manifestations of the Spirit would be encouraged. I did not know how to be the orchestra leader in the gathered community in such a meeting. I was torn by different directions from strong prophetic types who dogmatically put forth their revelations of direction for the congregation. I am truly indebted to two friends who greatly helped me in this regard. Here are some principles.

A leader needs to experience many meetings where the right governing models are experienced. This will greatly aid him in moving into governing Holy Spirit meetings. I learned from my friend Mike Bickle that the head leader must never give up his governing leadership to strong, domineering, prophetic types. These folks may pray four hours a day and receive technicolor visions and accurate prophetic words, but the leader must not be intimidated by them. The LORD must be trusted for the gift of wisdom in interpretation and application. The leader must exercise faith for this ability. It is also well for the people to pray for and believe that their leader can be led by the Spirit and interpret His moving. A decently capable pastor-leader with a normally consistent devotional life in which he regularly meets with the LORD can learn to govern. Often the person with revelation does not have accurate interpretation and application. The LORD desires that prophetic types would see their need to be submitted to governmental pastors and apostles. They are not an island unto themselves.

Instruction must be given to the congregants, especially those who prophesy regularly, that no directional words should be given publicly without first passing them by the elders – i.e., elders who have prophetic discretion (1 Corinthians 14:29-32) – who are governing the service that week. Also, words of rebuke or correction should be discerned by the governing leaders before they are given publicly to the congregation. In this way you will avoid unnecessary confusion. Of course, personal corrective words should be given privately and only after a pastoral person agrees and is present with the person who is to receive them. We made this a rule for all such personal directional words. With practice, the leader will sense where the LORD's balance is. The flock will not be tossed back and forth with every wind of prophetic direction. It is especially good when a plurality of elders develops this governing wisdom together. My pastor friend gave me the example of the spiritual leader governing a service or meeting as the one who draws together the prophetic flow, interprets and applies it, and gives the people understanding of what is happening. This produces confidence and security in the flock. He also teaches the flock how to be in a receptive mode to the Holy Spirit speaking in prophecy or visions.

Gifts and Anointing

Why is it important to grow and allow for the flow of the Holy Spirit's gifts and manifestations? It is because it is an essential part of New Covenant celebration, witness, and small group life. It is the anointing that breaks the yoke of bondage from people; the manifestations of the Spirit are types of the anointing. Because we can only do the LORD's work by his Spirit empowering, we have found that structuring our gatherings so that the Spirit is free to move has been a major reason for our spiritual growth.

The gifts of the Spirit are very useful in personal outreach in the contexts of serving lost people. When we are sharing the Good News of the Kingdom, words of wisdom and knowledge (prophecy) can reach the heart quickly. Ability through the Holy Spirit can cut through facades. John Wimber tells the story of riding on a 747 jet seated across from a business man. When he looked at him, he saw the word "adultery" written across his forehead. He was prompted to speak to him and tell him what the LORD had shown him. This led to weeping, repentance, and a commitment to Yeshua. This type of example could be repeated over and over. We all know the experience where the LORD changes our circumstances in order for Him to perform His purposes through us. Once in missing a train, I knew that I was called to share with someone on the next train. I was prompted to sit in a particular seat by the window and wait for the one the LORD had chosen. An open minded Orthodox Jew sat next to me. We had a wonderful dialogue, and it was obvious to me that it was a divine appointment. The LORD will lead us in what to say. We do not have to fear. Some will allow us to pray for their healing, and others will allow us to pray concerning a problem they may be having. When the LORD answers prayer or heals by the gift of healing, there is new openness.

The gifts of the Spirit, especially words of wisdom and knowledge, are very useful in counseling. Sometimes the counselor may have a prophecy or a vision that shows the roots of a hindrance to growth in the counselee's life. After prayer, a leap forward is achieved whereas weeks of counseling seemed to bring little progress. Wisdom can enable discernment when a counselee does not really desire to change. The motives of the heart can be uncovered. The ministry of deliverance and inner healing is greatly aided by prophecy, visions, and wisdom – both by the counselors, deliverance team members, and the person receiving deliverance. In Chicago, I found that a season of praying in tongues before deliverance would yield ideas of what the problem was and how to go on. Sometimes such ideas were prophetic insights into the person's past – much to their great amazement! Deliverance ministry is best accomplished in a team context. Members of the team may receive wisdom at various times when there is a lull in progress and direction. The supernatural work of the Spirit in inner healing and deliverance can take months or even years off the counseling process. Inner healing is simply receiving the healing power of the cross (the sacrifice of Yeshua) for the traumatic wounds and memories of the past. It enables the full forgiveness toward those who did the wounding, in the sense that bitterness is removed and our heart for those who did us wrong is truly for their repentance and redemption. It is important that congregations not produce ingrown self-preoccupation in their ministries of inner healing. There is a temptation to be too introspective (naval gazing) and focus on self, rather than on others. Also, care must be taken to not compromise with foreign, un-Scriptural healing methods. However, when the emphasis is on the power of the cross and resurrection to heal and deliver, progress may be rapid. The gifts of the Spirit are wonderful tools to enable people to leave the spiritual hospital bed and to become fruitful members of the hospital staff. Everyone needs some outpatient care at times, but our lives should show forth the power of Yeshua to deliver. Rather than being a manifestation of eternal therapy, our lives should manifest eternal life. A victorious life here and now is possible!

Governing the Small Group

The small group meeting is the primary place to see the kind of Holy Spirit structured gathering spoken of in 1 Corinthians 14 where one has a hymn, one has a prophecy, and another has a tongue and interpretation. A faithful person who loves the LORD can trust that what he or she receives in times of worship is the speaking of the LORD to them. When the Holy Spirit is moving in such a meeting, it is most exciting. The group leader in this context is called to draw out the shy and to tone down the domineering. He will need to establish that he is governing the meeting, not other strong personalities. If he does not do this, others will be discouraged and drop out. People will not feel protected or safe in allowing the Spirit to move freely through them. He must interpret the flow of the Spirit in the meeting and give people a sense of order. That which is fleshy should be gently and lovingly corrected. However, the genuine will be accentuated so it will be more predominant in the group. In governing, he could say things like, "Let's take these last three messages and see how they fit together." He may rephrase the most important points. He could also say, "Bill, I don't believe that this is where the Holy Spirit is taking us now; please hold this insight and see if it will fit in later." In praying for healing, he needs to make sure that no one speaks words that lay a guilt trip on the seeker like, "It is your lack of faith." Of course there is a lack of faith; why else would the person need prayer support! Revelations of bitterness or sin as hindering healing should be spoken privately by taking the person aside and only revealing it to the group with permission. Only those who are more proven in their gifts should be allowed to bring weighty corrective words like this. The group leader is the orchestra conductor under the Holy Spirit's direction.

In personal ministry contexts, it is important that the one who is ministering not be dogmatic. Words such as, "Thus saith the LORD" should be avoided. The people ministered to should be taught the freedom to be able to say, "I do not have a sense of confirmation" or, "This does not fit." There should not be condemnation for the ministering person either. This person can say, "I sense the LORD telling me _____. Does this fit?" Only violations of the teaching of the written Scriptures can be a source for clear and unyielding correction.

Governing in the Weekly Celebration

The main celebration of the whole community cannot be run as a 1 Corinthians 14 meeting. It is too large. Only a few could really share. However, this does not mean that there is no place for Holy Spirit manifestations. The flow of the service should be under the elders who lead that day. There is submission to the senior leader. The worship leader, those with prophetic words, and all others must submit to his governing authority in the service (or a plurality of elders who sit up front to judge and direct together). One common error in congregational life is that the worship leader, or people who believe they are prophetic, judge the governing of the service by the leader. Sometimes their judgments are so strong that they exercise negative faith and actually produce an atmosphere that is a spiritual force to trip up the leader. We have simply decided that we are standing firm on the principle of submission to the governing leader, and we teach people to repent of their judgments. The person who is not responsible for the whole service will not see as the leader sees. It is usually pride that motivates a person to be judgmental or critical.

In spite of size limits in the larger gathering, we do make room for the exercise of the gifts. After years of experimentation, we have found an order that fits us. If it is helpful to you, please draw from it. Our service flows from a lighter, more upbeat time of praise to a more reverent and devotional period of worship. Sometimes there is a time of quiet or singing in the Spirit. Toward the end of the worship period, I usually announce that members of the congregation are free to bring out their prophecies and exhortations to encourage the Body. This is usually not for individual words of knowledge unless there is an exceptional word to demonstrate the LORD's saving presence and power. Such words are very important, and we should have a place for them. We allow words to be brought forth if they are approved by the service leader through private consultation during the worship. We have often seen the prophetic flow anticipate the message from the Scriptures for that day. I will usually allow only three words in a row before interpreting, integrating, and calling for a time of silence to apply these words to one's life. I believe that 1 Corinthians 14 calls, not for a limit to the number of words in a service, but the number given at a time. If we are to take words seriously, we must reflect on them. After I sense that the congregation has received its fill for the day, I end the prophetic flow period. I am not concerned that everyone has a chance. Over the course of months, the prophetic flow of the main service will usually include a core of 5-10% of the congregants who develop a public prophetic ministry.

After the message for the day, we have a time of ministry. Words of knowledge are delivered for people's needs or conditions before our ministry time begins. All the prayer teams that minister (cell group leaders and others) are encouraged to be open to the Spirit as they pray. We have seen amazing manifestations of the Spirit in our services. During the post message ministry time, manifestations sometimes occur when there has been an exceptional word or demonstration, whether during or after the prophetic flow.

My wife Patty ministers prophetically. Once on Rosh Hoshana, she was given a dramatic word for a man she had never met. She received that he was a homosexual transvestite actor. She also received his nickname and saw that he would come forward to publicly repent. Patty approached him privately, which led to his publicly coming for prayer. At another meeting my wife called a woman forward who had stomach cancer. She was prayed for, and later she testified of her healing. Once our worship leader's wife was led to come forward and pray for a woman who had just received prayer from a pastoral couple. This woman came up for prayer as a skeptic to show her friends that there was no power in the prayer ministry. Our leadership sister had a prophetic word that she had some kind of pain and problem in the lower abdomen. She asked if she could pray for her. The skeptic was amazed that this was identified, for she had a painful ovarian cyst. When she was touched at that spot for prayer, she fell under the power of the Spirit. When she arose, she prayed to receive Yeshua as LORD and Savior. There are countless stories like these. Often words of this nature will be more frequent for the lost or for other visitors. This fulfills the description in 1 Corinthians 14 of the lost person falling down and admitting that the LORD is in the midst of the congregation.

Learn to Govern

My advice to leaders is that they learn to govern small group meetings and celebration services that are open to Holy Spirit manifestations. Neither allow an anything goes free for all, nor preclude the moving of the Spirit through gifts because of lack of confidence. Instead, spend some time in a community that does this in a quality way where there are regular manifestations. A righteous leader will learn quickly in such a setting. Spend some time with the leaders of such a community to learn through dialogue.

It is important to prepare the congregation for the Spirit. When there is life in a congregation, there are often messes that have to be cleaned up. They need to recognize that there is no way that one can give freedom without at times that freedom being abused. There will be those who will give flaky words. Sometimes a guest will not listen to the admonition of "members only" being released into public ministry and will reject those giving governmental correction and enforcement. Our desire for an aesthetically pleasing order will be thwarted and sometimes the Spirit will be quenched. However, during the learning stages, correcting the abuses with loving firmness will be a great lesson to the flock. Their confidence will provide a context for more genuine manifestations. There will be occurrences that sometimes make us uneasy, yet are of the LORD, although we may not be used to it.

What about the comfort zone of the pagan visitor? First, we do encourage visitors to come. However, we ask our members to prepare visitors for what they may see and why. Yes, we have had flaky manifestations, people shrieking out in ways that the LORD did not ordain. Sometimes these are tests and challenges from the enemy to get us to squelch the real gifts. Visitors are usually more accepting than the members who worry about what the visitors might think. We do not believe that our service is our primary evangelistic vehicle. Our celebration is mostly for the building up of the disciples of Yeshua according to New Covenant teaching. Our work of serving the lost is primarily to take place where they are to be found! However, we have found that many more lost people have been won because the Holy Spirit is given freedom in our midst than if He were quenched. The Scriptures command us to not quench the Spirit and to not despise prophecy. Sometimes this means precluding some from bringing forth the same banal word every week. We want the prophetic to be a real encouragement. It is so in our midst. It has also been an effective witness to visitors who do not know Yeshua.

Building Faith through the Scriptures

A congregation that attracts is one where the people are victorious. In 2 Peter 1 we read that the LORD has given us His precious promises that we might participate in His divine nature. A community will not be empowered by the Spirit unless they have strong faith. A key to fruitful congregation life is found in emphasizing a quality, loving devotional life with the LORD that confesses all of His promises as true for every situation. Part of this devotional life is to learn these promises and praise the LORD for each promise as a manifestation of His loving character. We are to then acknowledge that these promises are true for us. The right response in circumstances of great trial and challenge is to praise the LORD and to lovingly recite His promises as true for the situation. We are to relate to the LORD, not in mechanical formulae, but in loving devotion. We are to lay hold of the promises for our needs out of this loving relationship. I believe that we should speak no word that is contrary to the Scriptures, not even euphemistically. Building faith in the Scriptures is a key to all He desires for us. The LORD watches over His Word to perform it; not one of His words falls to the ground.

The Psychology of a Worship Service

For many years I was quite familiar with the evangelical tradition of worship. I call it, "Stand up, sing a hymn, sit down, have an announcement, have a prayer, and sing another hymn." Then we do the offering, have a special music selection, and then hear the sermon. I do not believe that this is Scriptural. The LORD's intent is that we attain an intimacy with Him as a corporate Body in worship. There is a normal pattern for attaining this intimacy that is found in both liturgical traditions and in the best charismatic services. The pattern is unmistakable whether in the synagogue, the Episcopal, or the Lutheran service. It is parallel to the process of intimacy in marriage. The service begins with preparation and material that is not deeply intimate (praise songs, well-chosen psalms, etc.) and moves to greater and greater intimacy. In the height of intimacy, the hymns, songs or choruses are sung slowly and to the LORD – not about the LORD – in devotional outpouring. (For example, "I Love You LORD" and "You are My Hiding Place"). High worship and intimate devotion are attained after psychological preparation. This is why many interruptions in the worship flow, soulish exhortations ("Let's really let it out now," etc.) can stifle intimacy. Our experience of worship is a reflection of how the LORD psychologically made us. As in the ancient Temple, we began in the outer court. The songs of ascent are not as personal and intimate. As we approached the Temple the experience is deeper and more reverent. At the Temple, there first was the outer court experience. In the inner court, we hear high praise and worship. Only the High Priest entered the most holy place. In our worship services, we enter the Most Holy Place. In the Most Holy Place, we find such awesome power and love that silence is often the only response we can make. Our psychological progression fits the architecture of the Temple. Those who have real intimacy with the LORD often recognize this. When they lead a service, they will order the service this way. Yes, at times this pattern will change. At times we will be led in triumphant praise in the Inner Court. However, I do believe that what we have said here is the normal pattern. The experience that we seek in corporate worship is best facilitated if we move from happy praise songs, to deeper praise, and then to intimate worship songs. Many have found this to be true.

Our Great Hope

As we bring this book to a close, I want to encourage you to believe that the LORD's ideals in the Scriptures are possible. It is possible to see communities of faith that can multiply leaders, plant new communities, and win and serve lost people. May the LORD encourage you and give you greater wisdom as you apply yourself to be an instrument of that great prayer, "Thy Kingdom come; Thy will be done on earth as it is in heaven." Please avail yourself of the important material in the appendices.

Rites of Passage in Messianic Jewish Congregations

In a Messianic Jewish Congregation it is important for a leader to understand the rituals surrounding the key transition times of life: birth, puberty, marriage, and death. Knowing how to apply these Jewish customs in our Messianic Jewish context is crucial if you want to be in continuity and connection to the Jewish community. Rites of passage are significant ways of bringing a greater depth of spiritual meaning to the key events of human life. They are universal in ancient cultures.

Birth

Perhaps no event of human life so immediately reflects the wonder and mystery of the LORD's greatness and love than birth. The birth of a child is the occasion for reaffirming the covenant and committing ourselves to pass that covenant on to our children. In the Jewish and Scriptural tradition, this covenant is passed on to Jewish sons through covenant circumcision – the *b'rit mileh*. This covenant is found in Genesis 17. The son of Jewish parents will be responsible for carrying on the covenant, for he has the potential to become a family head. The father will determine the religious identity of the family. In a Messianic Jewish congregation, all children are dedicated to the LORD with prayer in the presence of witnesses. This is often and ideally done during the main service of the congregation. Jewish boys receive circumcision on the eighth day to commit them not only to the Kingdom of God, but to the LORD's specific Jewish calling for the people of Israel. The ceremony is a simple one. Genesis 17 is read, and blessings and prayers in thanksgiving to the LORD are offered. This affirms our thankfulness for the opportunity to carry out the commitment to the LORD's covenant purposes. Messianic Jews have four options for this ceremony. The hardest to come by is to find a traditional *mohel*, a person who does covenant circumcisions from the Jewish community. To find one that will participate in a Messianic Jewish service of circumcision, where the principles of the New Covenant are affirmed, is no easy task; but some will do the rite anyway. For many years at Beth Messiah Congregation, we had the service of a *mohel* who was very supportive of our community and actually loved our fervor and commitment.

The second option is to find a doctor who will do the circumcision in a home as part of the ceremony. The third is to do the ceremony in the hospital when the circumcision is done. Lastly, attempt to find a Messianic Jewish *mohel*, a difficult task indeed for there are only a few in the world. One that trained for us is now retired.

Bar and Bat Mitzvah or Ben and Bat B'rit

These ceremonies represent the right of passage during puberty. The passage to sexual physical adult years is marked by most cultures as a significant milestone. In Judaism, the child is raised to be willing to embrace the covenant of the LORD, for at this age he can produce children. He must take full responsibility for moral behavior. Until the arrival of Reform Judaism, young women were not *bat mitzvah* (daughter of the covenant).

We believe that the years before puberty provide a quality opportunity for parents and the congregation to provide significant training for the child in the Scriptures. This includes teaching the responsibility of living according to our callings in the Body of the Messiah, whether we are Jew or Gentile. At Beth Messiah, the young person participates in our normal service. He or she reads from the Torah in Hebrew and English. The young person also gives a short speech professing their commitment of loyalty to the covenants. If they are Jewish, they commit to loyally follow Yeshua and to be part of the LORD's purposes for Jewish people. If they are not Jewish, they profess to be loyal to the LORD's purposes for them as part of the seed of Abraham through their commitment to Yeshua. This includes being committed to their part in seeing the good news of the Kingdom preached in all nations and to seeing Israel made jealous and come to know the Messiah. The ceremonies for our young people are otherwise the same. We have published a primer for young people based on *Growing to Maturity*. The young person is taught Hebrew, Jewish life, and most of all New Covenant principles of an intimate walk with Yeshua. Special times with the parents explaining their faith and the ways of the LORD are very significant. A willing young person can make a great leap forward in growth if this is handled well. Resources such as *Jewish Roots*, the *Growing to Maturity Primer*, and traditional materials for *bar* and *bat mitzvah* are helpful in putting together a program. The Jewish Rabbi's guide, the *Madrickh*, contains the traditional ceremony.

Weddings

Messianic Jewish weddings are quite common today. Most have tailored the traditional Jewish wedding ceremony by adding New Covenant material. The Jewish wedding is full of ancient symbolism. The couple makes a blood covenant together through the Jewish symbolism. As a symbol of coming under the household protection of the groom, the woman comes under the Hupah. Arnold Fruchtenbaum published one of the first examples of a Messianic Jewish version of the ceremony in his *Hebrew Christianity*. The traditional ceremony can be found in the daily Jewish Prayer Book, the Siddur, and in the Rabbi's guide, the *Madrickh*.

Death

The Jewish funeral tradition is significantly more humane than many western traditions. This is because the mourner does not provide for the funeral guests but the friends provide for the mourner. The tradition of saying *Kaddish* – a prayer of praise to the LORD in the face of loss and the affirmation of the hope for His Kingdom – is very comforting and appropriate. In addition, the mourning periods of seven intense days, a month of less intense mourning, and then the completion of 11 months of less intense mourning, enables the person to really face the loss and to grieve in a way that heals. With the addition of New Covenant material, Messianic Jewish funerals can be very meaningful. Indeed, the clarity of our hope in the resurrection based on the resurrection of Yeshua is very crucial and helpful. *Jewish Roots* gives more information on this. The traditional Jewish funeral is found in the Rabbi's guide, the *Madrickh*.

APPENDIX II

Handling Larger Conflicts and Factions

There are times when conflicts in a congregation "get out of hand." Factions of discontent, grumbling, and unfair complaints may form contrary to the Scriptures. At other times, a leader or leadership may lose credibility either by sin or by simply making multiple leadership mistakes. Often in the latter situation, congregants break covenant in the way they handle the issues. When a large faction forms, we often find it difficult to sort out how much of the problem is due to leadership issues and how much is due to the sin of the people who form a faction. I have experienced all kinds of problem situations in many major conflicts in congregations we oversee.

Frequently, local leadership is not credible enough to solve the problem of such factions. Having walked through several of these situations with very different outcomes, I have developed principles for those who handle various types of conflict. It is best if a team of leaders (two or three) is called in to handle situations where there are potentially damaging factions. They should be mature elders who are trained in their judicial responsibilities. Their involvement will require the ability to investigate and to weigh evidence and testimony. They need the strength of character to render a just and loving decision. At best, reconciliation will occur. At worst, the documentation of the truth and their judicial finding and direction will be recorded for those who want to know the truth and want to do what Scripture requires concerning the people involved.

Here are the key steps in such situations. First, it is important to organize a group of intercessors who will pray before and during the proceedings. We must be aware of the fact that we are dealing with spiritual warfare (not just flesh and blood) when we deal with such situations. Second, the congregation should be told well in advance that there is a meeting taking place so that they will have adequate time for their preparation. All who are part of having either given or received information on the complaints should be called to come to this meeting. Of course the meeting should especially include all who have formed a faction. Time should also be scheduled for all those who have serious concerns but have not shared these concerns with others.

The Use of a Questionnaire

It is good to have all who have been part of sharing their concerns, or receiving complaints, fill out a questionnaire. This can be handed out at the beginning of the meeting or ahead of time. Often we will find that some of the concerns and desires expressed by different members of a faction are contradictory. Questionnaires will sometimes lead to individual interviews. Have coffee and snacks at the meeting place. There will be times of joint meeting and individual interviews. Let each fill out their names, addresses, and phone numbers. We recommend that this questionnaire include the following:

1) What are your private offenses with the leader or leadership by which you believe that they are Scripturally disqualified for leadership or in need of significant correction?

2) What are your private offenses with the leader or leadership that do not disqualify the leader or leaders?

3) What are publicly committed offenses, if any, that you believe disqualify the leader or leadership? Name other witnesses to this.

4) What are serious public offenses that, from your view, do not disqualify the leader or leadership? Please name other witnesses to this.

5) What do you wish to see accomplished by this process (i.e., leaders removed, repentance and reconciliation while keeping the present leadership, reconciliation with a change of leadership etc.)?

6) Do you believe that this congregation is from the LORD and is meant to survive? If so, what should be done to enable its survival?

These questions lead the person to make their concerns explicit while they are led, not only to criticize, but to also think of constructive solutions.

In congregations that have an appeal process when things get out of hand, the issues of covenant will be easier to handle. The appeal process increases fairness potential in such situations and provides a process that removes excuses for non-covenantal behavior in handling disputes.

The Meeting Schedule

The meeting schedule should be prepared with time allotted for private testimony, with objections from those who desire to voice concerns but have not become part of the group. The meeting should begin with a teaching on the nature of covenant and the Scriptural way to handle disputes (especially Matthew 18:15ff.). After the teaching, there should be an opportunity to repent for those who wrongly shared their concerns with each other before they had shared with leadership or appealed to the higher judiciary. Any who violated Matthew 18 should clearly see it from the presentation. We are aware that sometimes leaders are so controlling and difficult that they greatly tempt their members to break covenant, but this will come out during testimony. Those who have shared their concerns will eventually hear the conclusions of the elders as to the accuracy of the accusations that have been mutually shared. Repenting for covenant breaking does not mean that the leaders are exonerated. This is only the first step for proper dealing with the issues. If a leader or leaders of the faction become known, it is good to have them testify first. Sometimes abusive leaders avoid correction by simply dismissing the people who complain due to covenant rule breaking. This is wrong.

The elders who are judging the case may sit at a table together. At another table, witnesses may be called. The proceedings should be taped. Each witness should tell his story. After each witness, corroborating witnesses may be called. One charge at a time must be identified and dealt with. The Scriptural rules of evidence (in the mouth of two or three witnesses) must be followed. Direct testimony establishes the truth unless there is conflicting direct testimony. However, several who report the same type of situation may also establish the truth.

After the testimonies, the accused may rebut this testimony and bring their witnesses. In addition, they may bring charges against people (which were not dealt with earlier) that may explain their actions. However, it is important that the leaders not bring charges that are private counseling matters unknown to the rest of the group. This should be handled privately (at least at first) and may lead to a withdrawal of accusations. If it is appropriate, these issues may then be brought forward. Accusations may be invalidated or withdrawn by such issues. Such hidden information may clearly exonerate a leader from charges of unfairness. His decisions of removing people from positions, for example, may be based on this private knowledge. The accuser uses the cloak of confidentiality to make a charge believable that otherwise would be seen as false charges.

When the full airing of the testimonies has ended, the judges retire to discuss and render a decision. Those that will not follow their decision as a court of appeal are in sin.

Sometimes both the leaders and the people are in the wrong – in different proportions. There can be mutual repentance at times without levels of sin or error that would require leadership removal. Sometimes leaders will have to be removed because of the level of sin or because of such incompetence that trust cannot be reestablished.

Three Case Studies

At this point it would be appropriate to recount three cases of judicial process where severe conflict had become spread in the congregation. The first concerns Beth Messiah congregation.

Case #1

In this situation, I submitted to a group of outside elders. A faction of disgruntled people had formed. Their unity was primarily because they were unhappy with the elders. Some did not agree with the eldership model of government. Others had a different vision for the congregation, at least in some regards. Others were hurting or unstable and projected their inner hurts from their past onto authority. In this situation, they had formed a faction. The Beth Messiah elders thought that the faction included about a dozen, but twenty-five out of a membership of ninety (weekly attendance of 130) came to a meeting. After meeting from 7pm until 1am, none of the charges were established. The elders sitting in judgment declared that those present had formed an unholy faction and called on them to repent. They upheld a former disfellowship decision that was at least part of the occasion for the faction to gel. After this decision was made, all of those in the faction left the congregation. None repented, but they lost credibility with the rest of the congregation.

However, because of the strong confirmation and decision of the outside elders, the congregation's elders gained the trust of the rest of the members. The congregation began to grow with a new unity of vision and ethical standards. Those that remained favored the government and the vision. Often, those who form a faction claim to speak for all, but they only represent a minority in disagreement with the majority. Over the years Beth Messiah became, for a season, the largest Messianic Jewish congregation in the world.

Case #2

The next example is one where the leader was basically acquitted, but he needed to repent for errors made out of inexperience. In this situation, the leader sometimes was misunderstood because of poor communication. Some thought that the leader was disfellowshipping others without due process. However, he was only warning some to be careful of others who were not stable members of the Body. There was no official decision made against them. He had also involved the elders in concerns about a business because many members worked at a company owned by a former leader. Sometimes he received reports about this business in a non-covenantal way. However, accusations of cultic control and serious sin could not be sustained. The leader was corrected, but the far more serious sin of grossly false accusations from others also had to be corrected. The leader was found to be qualified. After those who could not trust the leader left, the congregation attained a new unity and began to grow in quality of worship and numbers.

Case #3

In another situation, a faction had formed against a leader who also was on a learning curve. Two judicial meetings were necessary. In the first, accusations of gross sin were not sustainable. However, the leader did mistreat members when he believed that he was the brunt of false accusation and mistreatment. Anger and rejection was projected. A faction of about fifteen formed in his congregation. Testimony led to mutual repentance. The leader repented for his failures. All but two couples repented of their sin in forming the faction and breaking covenant standards for handling disputes. One couple left the congregation, admitting wrong in the procedure, but they were still not able to trust the leadership. The other couple remained with the exhortation to work out their concerns over time. This was a mistake. The resolution seemed completed. However, six months later a core of leaders in training along with one elder resigned. They had shared their complaints against the leader with each other without appealing to the outside elder leadership. Because these were the only leaders under the head leader, though they were only in training, their resignation dealt a credibility blow to the leader of the congregation that could not be resolved. After all, these were the ones picked by the leader as the best candidates for leadership from the congregation. When outside elders came to seek to resolve the issues, the following resulted. First, the leaders in training admitted that they had sinned in the way they handled their concerns. The extra-local elders interviewed all of the remaining people and found that the great majority no longer trusted him to be the pastor of the congregation. The only alternative was to seek to bring healing, mutual repentance, and to form a fellowship under a temporary coordinating committee, as there were no elders for the functions of a fully operating congregation.

Closing a Congregation in a Covenant Way

Even where a congregation cannot be rescued, it is well worthwhile to close a congregation in a covenantal and orderly way, seeking the healing and future success of all who were involved. In this regard, it is well to see that mutual repentance, forgiveness, and reconciliation take place on a personal level.

I hope that these thoughts are helpful for congregations that undergo severe conflicts. Judges must seek love and justice. This means they must be truly fair to both leaders and followers. They must judge by Scriptural standards and evidence, not prejudice of any kind.

One thing we have recently learned in planting congregations is the importance of having adequate feedback for the planting pastor and those elders to whom they are accountable in planting, even if those elders are not locally available. In planting stages we recommend an advisory and feedback board of the first members. This board should understand that it is temporary and does not have authority for making the decisions. In a monthly or twice monthly meeting, this board can give the planter feedback on all areas of congregational life. They should make written reports monthly to the extra-local elders. This board may later include deacons. Ultimately, when a board of elders is in place, this board will dissolve. Sitting on this board should not be understood as leading to eldership. The value of this board is to give feedback and to see that communication channels are kept open. Developing problems can thus be nipped in the bud before they get out of hand.

As we deal with the issues of discipline, we need to emphasize the danger of a growth of negativism, judgmental-ism, and criticism in a congregation. Even when leaders are doing no significant wrong and are leading adequately, this spirit can grow up. As people exercise judgment, which is a strong negative faith, leaders will sometimes find themselves powerless, acting befuddled and making mistakes they would not ordinarily make. This is why teaching faith, emphasizing unity of vision, and dealing with problems in covenant is so important. Remember also the previous exhortations we have given on spiritual warfare and prayer for these situations.

APPENDIX III

Messianic Jewish Worship, Priesthood, and Communion

Christians frequently ask one another how they enjoyed the worship service. Did they get something out of the worship or the preaching? The Jewish tradition of prayer is not about getting something out of it. The same prayers are prayed daily. It is rather about fulfilling an intercessory responsibility for the sake of Israel and that Israel's redemption would lead to the redemption of the world. The Jewish prayer service is built around identification with the sacrificial system. When the Temple existed, the limited but important synagogue liturgy was a way of identifying with the sacrifices taking place in Jerusalem. This was especially important in the Jewish communities of the Diaspora. The *Amidah* or *Shemoneh Esreh* (Standing Prayer or The Eighteen Benedictions) were especially understood as identification with sacrifices since the *Kedusha*, or the recitation of the "holy, holy, holy" from Isaiah 6, was Isaiah's experience in the Temple or the place of sacrifice. The idea that the Temple preserved the world in existence until the Messiah would come is found in Rabbinic literature. Prayer, study, and good deeds were seen as still performing this function after the Temple was destroyed, but the prayer was in explicit identification with the sacrifices. When one studies the Jewish prayer tradition, one finds a remarkable Scriptural content and theology permeating the prayers. This leads us to our general approach to Rabbinic Judaism or the Jewish traditional heritage of prayer and living. Paul exhorts us in Romans 13 to give honor to whom honor is due. The Scriptures also exhort us to honor our fathers and our mothers. This means that we are duty bound to honor that which is good, beautiful, and true in the Jewish heritage as measured by the Scriptures, especially in the New Covenant. We are to honor what is good and discard what is not good. However, even if we study the basics of the Jewish heritage, the issue of what we practice is still by the Spirit. There are many good things that are to be honored that the LORD may not lead us to embrace. So again, here is our three fold approach. First, we are called to study the heritage of our people as a necessary part of honoring them. Second, we are to honor what is good and to honestly be truthful about what is not good and discard it. Third, we are to seek the leading of the Spirit concerning what we are to incorporate according to our circumstances in establishing the Gospel.

The Jewish prayer tradition from the first century provided the basic elements for the classic Christian communion service. The classic book on this subject is by Louis Bouyer entitled *Eucharist* (which means "thanksgiving" and is the Christian historical name for communion). He argues that the communion service of classical Christianity goes back to the synagogue and probably had apostolic origins. It included (and we can still see these elements) several of the benedictions of the *Shemoneh Esreh*, the *Kedusha* or the "holy, holy holy" recitation and prayer going back to Isaiah 6, along with the phrases on the angelic beings in their worship. It includes the two preliminary blessings before the *Sh'ma* and the confession of our commitment to love the LORD alone. The first of these preliminary blessings declares the LORD as the Creator of life and all things. The second declares the LORD's love for Israel – and in the Christian revision His love for Christians. However, the major change is that instead of identification with the sacrifices of the Temple, the

Christian liturgy leads to the celebration of the sacrifice of Yeshua by partaking of the bread and wine as the body and blood of Yeshua. The ancient tradition of the Christian community believed in a release of power in the very celebration, the claim of the people, and the territory for the LORD, wherever the sacrifice of Yeshua was celebrated. Of course, the Christian community took into the liturgy both Passover and Yom Kippur symbolism, and Bouyer notes that a Passover form of the Jewish Grace after meals is also perceived in the liturgy. Finally, of course, the Christian community proclaims warnings before partaking, self-examination, and confession of sin since participation in the communion is serious business. We really do participate in His death and resurrection anew, which was first experienced in water immersion. Thus 1 Corinthians 11 is an important part of the liturgy, as well as the confession of faith in both the Father and the Son in lieu of the *Sh'ma*. This is amazing teaching and the history is unknown to most Messianic Jews and Christians.

In addition, I would add that in New Covenant worship, we are enjoined in John 5 to honor the Son as we honor the Father. How can we do this? One of my proposals is that communion be a much more significant and regular part of our gathering for worship. In addition, we should understand our gathering as first for the purpose of ministering to the LORD and engaging in intercession. The Communion can be a wonderful combination of the ancient Jewish foundations that became part of the ancient Christian liturgy – but in a Messianic Jewish context. This allows for Jewish foundational content to be put back in a more recognizable form, while making the central message conveyed to be what the LORD has done for us in the Messiah and our participation in His body and blood.

I would also note that many passages of the New Testament are liturgical hymns and faith confessions. This includes Philippians 2:6-11, 1 Corinthians 15:3-7 in the confession of Yeshua's resurrection, Hebrews 1:1-3 on the revelation in the Son, Col. 1:15-21 ff. on the nature of the Son, and so much more. In addition there are many

New Covenant benedictions, and we are not limited to the Aaronic benediction from Numbers 6. Passages of praise to the Father and the Lamb in the book of Revelation are also quite powerful. These are great New Covenant Scripture passages that fit very well into our Jewish worship service, and they should be much more frequently used.

Let us teach our people their intercessory responsibilities and have great contemporary worship and great historically based liturgy – that is, as we are led by the Spirit.

APPENDIX IV

Recent Books for Leadership Training

There is no need to give bibliography for the following books. A Google search on Amazon and Barnes and Noble can easily enable you to locate them. These books are mostly from the business world, but the universal principles in them are amazingly helpful.

1) Stephen Covey's *The Seven Habits of Highly Effective People*. This is the best book I know on the habits and self-management of a leader.

2) Stephen Covey's *The Speed of Trust*. This is an amazing read on how to build trust in an organization – and how this enables you to be much more fruitful.

3) Jim Collins' *Good to Great*. This is the best book on how to build great organizations that lead into the next generation. Shared leadership that follows the headship and plurality model, argued in the book, is his model for business corporations.

4) Thom S. Rainer's *Breakout Churches*. This fine book applies the lessons of *Good to Great* as applied to building congregations.

5) Kerry Patterson's *Crucial Conversations*. This is a very powerful book on how to have those difficult conversations that are necessary to address major issues, where the stakes are high, and to work toward good conclusions. It gives leaders courage to do the hard task of engaging difficult conversations and is a key to building trust in the team and the community.

6) Kerry Patterson's *Crucial Confrontations*. This is a fine book extending the themes of the above book.

7) Dallas Willard's *The Divine Conspiracy*. A passionate and powerful statement on the call to disciple, along with clarity on just what it is and how it is done.

In addition, I want to recommend three of my books as especially important for leaders in their congregational work. You can find them from our office, Lederer, or Destiny Image. All of my books are relevant, but these more so.

1) *Growing to Maturity*. This is the most widely used book for basic doctrine and discipleship in the Messianic Jewish movement. It is in a new 2012 edition and has now been in print for 30 years. It is in English, Hebrew, Russian, and Spanish.

2) *The Irrevocable Calling*. This is a short book that presents the case for a distinctive call of Jewish disciples of Yeshua to live and identify as part of their people and why. It is crucial in seeing that Jews who believe in Yeshua do not give up their Jewish identity and assimilate.

3) *Jewish Roots: A Foundation of Biblical Theology*. This book was one of the two foundational classics in laying out a Messianic Jewish theology of the Scriptures. The other was David Stern's *Messianic Jewish Manifesto*, now under the title of *Messianic Judaism*. The theology of these two books is very similar. They have both been in print more than 25

years. *Jewish Roots* is now in a fully revised 2012 edition that takes into account recent advances in scholarship.

(Endnotes)

1   *Charisma* provided updated research on mega-churches in June 2014 here: http://www.charismamag.com/spirit/church-ministry/20667-did-you-know-these-9-things-about-people-who-attend-megachurches

2   See www.messianiclifeonline.org

3   See www.mjbi.org

4   See Rudolph's works "Congregational Government and Leadership" and "Disputes, Discipline, and Reconciliation in the Body of Believers: A Handbook of Procedure and Theology" and "Kingdom Government and Spiritual Gifts here: http://www.genesisobservatory.us/ohev/Menus%20&%20Pages/The%20Rabbis%20Corner/Papers.html

Made in the USA
Lexington, KY
02 May 2015